PASS

A Guide to
Creating Physically Active School Systems

Carol M. Ciotto; Dr. Marybeth H. Fede

authorHOUSE®

AuthorHouse™
1663 Liberty Drive
Bloomington, IN 47403
www.authorhouse.com
Phone: 1-800-839-8640

Published by AuthorHouse   05/14/2015

ISBN: 978-1-4969-3108-5 (sc)
ISBN: 978-1-4969-3145-0 (e)

Library of Congress Control Number: 2014921972

Print information available on the last page.

Table of Contents

SECTION I: PHYSICALLY ACTIVE SCHOOLS

This section will provide readers with information about the components of a physically active school, why schools should provide physical activity programs and the physical and cognitive benefits for students who participate in such a program.

This chapter will help the reader to make important connections between mind and body in order to make a lasting commitment for creating a physically active environment, and help the readers learn to advocate for the program, and communicate and collaborate with the stakeholders.

A) Defining a physically active school system: What does it look like? What are the components?

B) Who is involved and what are their roles?

C) Benefits of PASS- Why do we need PASS?

This chapter will provide a framework for schools to follow in order to implement physical activity throughout the school system.

A) Make a Commitment to become a physically active school system (getting everyone on board).

B) Identifying Resources to help define the mission, goals, and action plan for PASS

C) Collaborate with the stake holders (administration, faculty/staff, students, parents & Community- those interested in seeing improvement in the school environment).

D) Develop an action plan: Identify steps needed to create PASS (needs assessment, elements for implementation, create a time line, etc.)

E) Promote PASS initiative (advocacy: Social Media, Newsletter, District & School websites, etc.)

E) Motivational techniques among stake holders (provide rewards and incentives for participation, promotional materials that build excitement)

F) PASS Kick off: This will signify the start of the implementation of a physically activeschool system.

SECTTION II: WHAT DOES PASS LOOK LIKE?

This section will deal with the various components of a physically active school system. Each chapter will look at parts of the school day and provide specific examples of where and how physical activity can be imbedded. (See Appendix B for an example of an activity from each of the following chapters)

This chapter will give hands on before and after school activities, such as the Walking School Bus to get students active, focused, and ready to learn.

This chapter will give hands on During school activities, such as the Brain Dance to get students active, focused, and ready to learn.

This chapter will give hands on Recess activities, such as the Yoga Recess to get Students active, focused, and ready to learn after lunch.

This chapter will give hands on Family/Community activities, such as the FFF Night (Fun, Family, Fitness Night) in order to get parents and children collaborating on their health and wellness.

SECTION III: RESOURCES AND EXCERPTS FROM THE FIELD

This section will provide readers with a variety of resources and examples of various activities that are being utilized in schools across the nation.

This chapter will provide examples of successful PASS programs that currently exist in various school systems throughout the country. Activate Southington, Southington Public Schools, CT.

About the Authors

Carol M. Ciotto

Carol M. Ciotto is an Associate Professor at Central Connecticut State University in the Department of Physical Education and Human Performance Department and has been teaching in the teacher preparation field for the past 11 years. Prior to teaching at CCSU she spent 23 years serving as a physical education teacher, an assistant principal and a principal in the public school setting. She holds a BS in Physical Education, an MS in School Administration and a 6th Year Supervisory/Administrative Certificate. Carol has served on the Connecticut Association of Health, Physical Education, Recreation and Dance (CTAHPERD) Executive Council as a Vice President of Physical Education, Vice President of Dance and the 2013-2014 President. She is currently the Executive Director of the Society of Health and Physical Educators (SHAPE America) Eastern District and is a member of the Connecticut Cadre of Physical Education Trainers. Carol has presented at various conferences at the state, regional, national and international levels over the past 34 years and has published peer reviewed articles in various educational journals. Throughout her career she has received several awards and recognitions for her service to the profession and her excellence in teaching including Teacher of the Year. Carol has a true passion for teaching and learning and is committed to continuous service to the field.

Dr. Marybeth H. Fede

Marybeth H. Fede Ed.D is an Associate Professor of Exercise Science at Southern Connecticut State University. Alumni of SCSU she holds a BS in Physical Education (79), MS in Human Performance

(86), 6th year in School Health (87), and she also earned her EdD in Adult Education from Nova Southeastern University (09). She has been teaching at Southern as an adjunct and now as a full time professor in the teacher preparation field for the past 27 years. She is on the Board of Directors and is the secretary of the Alumni Association. She also serves the professional organization: the Connecticut Association of health, Physical Education, Recreation and Dance (CTAHPERD), as the conference program coordinator. Marybeth has presented at various conferences at the state, regional, national and international levels over the past 15 years and has published peer reviewed articles in various educational journals. She has two beautiful children, Jacquelyn, 25 and John, 24. She is an active person, who practices what she preaches and loves to dance, golf and ski, not necessarily in that order.

Introduction

We began writing a book because we want to see all children succeed. We teach college students how to become physical educators and in doing so we get much pleasure and joy when our students become contributing members of society by becoming physical education teachers. We also feel it is our responsibility to teach our students to be effective physical educators, and in this vein, we encourage them to become pro-active; to reach out to the classroom teachers; to incorporate curriculum related material into the PE program; to physically educate ALL students; to start before and after school programs; to help administrators, faculty, parents, community leaders, and most importantly CHILDREN to make the important connection between physical activity and increased cognition, attendance, and decrease in behavior issues, not to mention the overall health benefits of being active which eventually leads to a decrease in childhood obesity. It is our intent to help all educators understand and be able to feel comfortable using the powerful tool of movement to enhance students' physical, emotional, spiritual, and cognitive fitness. It started as a guidebook for administrators and ALL educators. It has evolved into a bigger project where we are training several school districts throughout Connecticut in the PASS initiative. We eventually want the whole State and Nation to adopt the PASS philosophy and reap the benefits of happy, healthy, smart children!

Whether an administrator, faculty member, classroom teacher, or special area teacher, everyone wants to see their students' learning improve. Improved learning validates the roles and influences of educators and administrators. The purpose of this book is to assist educators in how to create a physically active school. Understanding the role physical activity and/or movement plays in the gymnasium and the classroom will contribute significantly to this effort. Movement helps to differentiate instruction, by increasing retention, motivation, attention and engagement in the learning process. It should be utilized for its full potential benefits in both the classroom and gymnasium.

The solution begins and ends with the decisions we make. Children are not getting as much physical activity as they should, despite the many benefits. It is important to establish good physical activity habits as early as possible. So how do we do that? By making physical activity and quality physical education a part of your school's culture by increasing the amount of physical activity students participate in, throughout the day, every day. It is critical that we take the steps now to educate and make a change in our student's lives to help them lead a healthier, more productive life.

It can be challenging to motivate students, especially when it comes to a lifestyle change. The most effective way to instill change is to make it simple and attainable. By imbedding physical activity as a part of the school's culture before, during and after school, children will more likely adopt it as a part of their everyday behavior. This book provides strategies and resources on how to create a physically active school with examples of activities and programs that can be incorporated throughout the school day. By providing opportunities for physical activity throughout the school day, students can bring this new behavior home and out into the community so we can all learn the importance of healthy behavior while improving cognition and academic success.

As a school professional, your role in implementing physical activity into your school begins with a commitment to build a healthier, more physically active school environment for the future of your students. The goal is for all children to get at least 60 minutes of moderate to vigorous physical activity every day, with at least 30 minutes attained at school (SHAPE America, 2014; ACSM, 2000). Schools are a key setting for students to get their 60 minutes of physical activity, given the amount of time spent there. Schools can provide a variety of strategies and approaches to help students become more physically active, that include quality physical education programs and opportunities within the school that increases access to physical activity for all students to be physically active not just during physical education class but throughout the day. Students can get most of their physical activity through a quality physical education program that is complemented by activities before, during, and after school, recess, physical activity breaks, intramural programs, interscholastic sports, and walking or biking to and from school. Schools play a key role in shaping the social and physical development of their students.

Many know the health-related benefits associated with being physically active, and now the field of exercise science can add brain power to the long list of tried and true benefits. Educators need to realize that all faculty and administrators are on the same side in fighting childhood obesity, reducing the onset of type II diabetes, and using exercise to combat behavior disorders instead of drugs, while at the same time raising test scores. Ratey (2008) refers to the good news as a revolution, so let us take up the cause and raise our heart rates, put our heads together, and pull out all the stops to give children the best chance to be smart, healthy contributing members of society, by providing them with a truly interdisciplinary, holistic education.

Chapter 1

What is PASS?

PASS, a Physically Active School System, is a program through which school districts can utilize opportunities for school-based physical activity that contribute to overall fitness and enhanced cognition and which can be broken down into four integral parts. First, there needs to be an understanding of the important connection between mind and body. Making this connection is crucial to the success of the program and on a bigger scale, to have an impact on childhood obesity. The positive effects of connecting physical activity to learning have been around for many years (Berg & Sady, 1983; McKenzie et al., 1996; Sallis & McKenzie, 1998; Stone, McKenzie, Welk, & Booth, 1998; U.S. Department of Health and Human Services [USDHHS] 2000). However, it wasn't until Ratey (2008) published his book, *Spark: the Revolutionary New Science of Exercise and the Brain*; that we have begun to take notice.

Second, cooperation among administrators (superintendents & principals), faculty (classroom teachers, physical educators, and other "special" subject areas), parents, and children needs to occur. Administrators need to be supportive of training for classroom teachers, so they are comfortable implementing informal, formal and content-rich physical activities in the classroom. They also need to recognize the importance of daily, quality physical education programs. These types of comprehensive programs not only provide health benefits for students, but can also reinforce the classroom curriculum, through such programs as the ABC's of Fitness (Katz, 2007) and Action Based Learning (Blaydes, 2000). There needs to be support of and cooperation among these groups in order for PASS to be successful.

Third, collaboration among legislators, institutions of higher education, community leaders, school administrators and parents needs to occur. Legislators need to provide opportunities for grants and service learning projects throughout their districts. Colleges and universities need to prepare their pre-service teachers to not only understand the benefits of physically active classrooms, but to be able to effectively implement a physically active program in their student teaching placement and eventually in their full-time employment. Partner with organizations (i.e. parks and recreation departments, youth development organizations, local governments, health service providers, faith-based organizations, and parents) to build communities around good nutrition, and positive and inclusive physical activity. Legislators need to provide policy change, incentives, enabling resources, guidance and support to this end.

Finally, it takes a village to raise one healthy child, and in that vein, a mass communication effort needs to take place to craft the message and image of physical activity and physically active learning as an expectation and a right! Advertise the good news regarding physical activity and learning, and the cooperation and collaboration that is taking place among the schools, community leaders, legislators, and parents for the success of their children and our future. Comprehensive school health and physical education programs are a good start, but as we know from past experience they are not enough on their own. Physically active classrooms, intramurals, before and after school programs, community outreach programs, and parks and recreation programs all have to work together to provide the most optimum experiences for children and adults to participate in physical activities.

In order for PASS to be successful the roles and responsibilities of the key stakeholders should be addressed. These individuals should have a vested interest in PASS the best approach is to include representatives from: school boards, administrators, school faculty and staff, students, parents, and community partners. Chapter Two will elaborate on who the key stakeholders are and their respective roles and responsibilities.

Having a solid understanding of the benefits of a PASS program and why it is needed will help the reader to make important connections between mind and body in order to make a lasting commitment for creating a physically active environment. Being physically active is important in combating hypokinetic diseases and certain types of cancer (United States Department of Health and Human Services USDHHS, 1996-present). We can now add to the long list of benefits of physical activity; increased cognition, focus, and overall readiness to learn. It is the intent of the authors, in this chapter, to help all educators understand and be able to feel comfortable using the powerful tool of movement to enhance students' physical, emotional, spiritual, and cognitive abilities.

Whether an administrator, faculty member, classroom teacher, or special area teacher, (Art, Music and Physical Education) everyone wants students test scores to improve and know that they contributed to it. These improved scores validate the roles and influence of educators and administrators. The purpose of this book is threefold: First to provide compelling information through a review of literature, for why movement needs to be incorporated into the school culture. Interviews with Pre K-12 educators to gather ideas and best practices for interdisciplinary teaching will be shared, along with an analysis of pre-existing data from state standardized test scores. Secondly the book will provide a framework on how to get started creating a physically active school system for administrators and educators. A variety of teaching strategies and techniques will be included in order to better understand the role physical activity plays in the classroom, which will in turn contribute significantly to improved cognition among students. Physical activity differentiates instruction, increases retention, motivation, attention and engagement in the learning process. Thirdly the book will provide a variety of activities that can be incorporated before and after school, during school, at home with the family and within the community.

The primary focus of this book will emphasize the importance of using physical activity to its full potential by all educators.

Although it is important that high quality physical education programs exist within a school, it is only the beginning to solving the childhood obesity problem and how sedentary we as a nation have become. With all the research being done about the effects of physical activity on focus, cognition, readiness to learn (California State Board of Education, 2007, Ratey, 2008), and armed with the fact that aerobic activity can actually help create new neurological pathways, and the Naperville, IL model, (Ratey, 2008) we now have proof that fit kids are smarter. We cannot over emphasize the importance of making the connection between the mind and body. How the information is disseminated is where the problem lies. History tells us that using the doom and gloom approach, the threat of disease, or even staving off diseases doesn't work. Educators have to change the Nation's story from the detrimental effects of a sedentary lifestyle to one about improved health and performance beginning with physical activity as the basis of the pyramid. Our social, emotional and spiritual health all depend on our physical health.

Americans have a million excuses not to be physically active, with the number one reason being not enough time. Other barriers to full engagement include but are not limited to technology, multi-tasking, denial, self-deception and it's easier not to! (CDC 2001) Educators need to understand the barriers and that it is not the stress that is bad, but rather the lack of recovery time that we don't allow ourselves or our students. We need to get students fully engaged. Stress is not the enemy, it is how we grow, get stronger, and produce energy. It is only when we fail to manage the recovery period properly that problems arise (Groppel, 2011). In this day and age of smart phones, I-pads, and information at our fingertips, we are so busy multi-tasking and trying to handle multiple stimuli; that we never really fully disengage. This is what is hazardous to our health and well-being. Making excuses and telling ourselves the wrong story may give us meaning and significance, but it prevents real change, becoming fully engaged and disengaged. You can make a difference one student at a time by understanding the barriers to full engagement. Including Gardner's (1999) eight multiple intelligences, and Glasser's (1998) five basic human needs in your teaching is a great way to reach all the very different individuals that make up your classes. Furthermore, Lengel & Kuczala's (2010) framework for movement in the classroom, Blayde's, (2000) action based learning, Katz's (2010) ABC's for fitness, brain breaks in the classroom, Gilbert's (2000), brain dance, Ratey's (2008), Naperville, IL model, and before and after school programs which lead to community involvement, are all available tools that can help achieve the mission. We need to arm ourselves with these tools, reframe the story, collect data, and disseminate the information to the classroom teacher, administrators, board of education members, parents and most importantly our students.

In order to understand the connection between the mind and the body, educators need to fully comprehend what physical activity/ movement is and the benefits of imbedding it throughout the day. According to Blaydes (2000) there are three distinctions of movement, that need to be addressed when reviewing brain research: 1) movement, 2) physical activity, and 3) exercise. Movement is the navigation of one's environment. Physical activity is any movement of the skeletal muscle that expends energy. Exercise is physical activity that is planned and repetitive, with an increase in physical fitness as the goal. The two aspects of movement that benefit learners most are physical fitness and use of kinesthetic activities to anchor academic concepts resulting in cognitive reinforcement. According to Blaydes (2000), "movement prepares the brain for optimal learning" (p. 2).

Early research dealing with physical activity and cognition showed that physical activity enriches the learning environment; physical fitness is positively related to academic performance, and aerobic fitness aids cognition (Diamond, 1998; Gage, 1999; Gardner, 1983; Jensen, 1998). More recent research has documented the positive benefits physical activity/movement and exercise, have on cognition. In 2008, Ratey introduced the world to *Spark: The New Revolutionary Science of Exercise and the Brain*. He began prescribing various types of physical activity and exercise to his patients as treatment for everything from anxiety, stress, and depression to Alzheimer's disease. He also researched the effect of aerobic exercise on academic performance. With regular and prolonged aerobic activity, such as brisk walking or bike riding, new neurological pathways in the brain are created, which benefit old and young alike.

Movement differentiates instruction, increases retention, motivation, attention and engagement in the learning process, and should be utilized for its full potential benefits in both the classroom and in the gymnasium (Lengel & Kuczala, 2010; Ratey, 2008). "The research confirms that students perform better in school when they are emotionally and physically healthy. They miss fewer classes, are less likely to engage in risky or antisocial behavior, concentrate more and attain higher test scores" (NASPE, 2011 p.1).

Exercise is also of extreme importance, as it improves learning on three levels: 1) it optimizes the mindset to improve alertness, attention, and motivation; 2) it prepares and encourages nerve cells to log in new information; and 3) it spurs the development of new nerve cells from stem cells in the hippocampus (Ratey, 2008). By addressing the need for more physical activity during the school day and its positive effect on cognition, attendance and behavior, society can begin to see the possibility of an end to the problems of childhood obesity, type 2 diabetes and declining test scores (Kelly, Kelly & Franklin, 2006; Cotman & Engresser-Cesar, 2002).

According to Lengel and Kuczala (2010), two important keys to improved cognition for educators to understand are the difference between implicit and explicit learning and certain principles the brain seeks out. First, explicit learning occurs on a very conscious level, often through reading, lecture, listening, discussion and work sheets. Second, implicit learning involves more neural pathways and sensory cues, which allow the brain to learn more quickly and remember more accurately. Implicit learning often occurs through movement, life experiences and emotions, and is the preferred way for the brain to acquire information. The brain seeks novelty and likes to operate from concrete experiences.

It tries to make meaning through questioning i.e., does this make sense? Emotions and the movement of the body and objects in the environment both contribute to an enhanced learning experience. Movement enhances the teaching/learning process in a variety of ways, including: improving brain function, increasing circulation, refocusing attention, enhancing episodic memory, reducing sitting time (which produces blood pooling and the release of melatonin), changing the brain chemically, providing breaks from learning, (as well as a motivational framework for learning and an opportunity for implicit learning), and stimulating neurogenesis (through prolonged aerobic activity). In addition, movement is the best available manager of state. State management refers to one's ability to manage the brain and body's physical, mental, and emotional states. By understanding the brains need to manage state the educator can better understand students' limited attention spans, their need to self-regulate mood, and the mind/body state that influences the process of meaning making (Hannaford, 1995; Jensen, 2000; Katz, 2007; Lengel & Kuczala, 2010; Ratey, 2008). Knowing this information and all of the other benefits that are associated with movement substantiates the need for physical activity and movement in the classroom (Kuczala, 2010).

Educators and administrators need to understand that from the time of birth we learned to roll over, crawl, walk, talk, and were given many accolades for these achievements. Upon entering school however, the tone changed and we were told to sit still and be quiet. This goes against everything our bodies need to do. Physical activity/movement, music, and novelty are relatively simple means to manage state, and help students make a much smoother transition to the very still and stifled environment in a school setting. As the teacher/facilitator it is important to understand and apply the five basic human needs (Glasser, 1965, 1998), the eight multiple intelligences (Gardner, 1999), and simple brain principles (Lengel & Kuczala, 2010) to the learning environment. Movement creates a joyful atmosphere in the classroom, and Kuczala (2010) provides a framework of movement for teachers to follow. He advocates six purposes for movement which include 1) preparing the brain, 2) providing brain breaks, 3) class cohesion activities, 4) support of exercise and fitness, 5) attaching kinesthetic activity to content and 6) movement-oriented content games (reviewing content). Overall, movement in the classroom helps to support relationships, relevance and/or meaning making, and rigor. Refer to Figure 1 to get a better idea of how to implement Kuczala's framework for movement model in the classroom, gymnasium, art, and/or music rooms. By focusing on the needs of every individual student, there is a greater likelihood of improved cognition.

It can be challenging to motivate students, especially when it comes to a lifestyle change. The most effective way to instill change is to make it simple and attainable. By imbedding physical activity as a part of the school's culture before, during and after school, children will more likely adopt it as a part of their everyday behavior. By providing opportunities for physical activity throughout the school day, students can bring this new behavior home and out into the community so we can all learn the importance of healthy behavior while improving cognition and academic success.

As a school professional, your role in implementing physical activity into your school begins with a commitment to build a healthier, more physically active school environment for the future of your students. The goal is for all children to get at least 60 minutes of moderate to vigorous physical activity every day, with at least 30 minutes attained at school (AAHPERD, 1975; ACSM, 2000). Schools are a key setting for students to get their 60 minutes of physical activity, given the amount of time spent there. Schools can provide a variety of strategies and approaches to help students become more physically active, that include quality physical education programs and opportunities within the school that increases access to physical activity for all students to be physically active not just during physical education class but throughout the day. Students can get most of their physical activity through a quality physical education program that is complemented by activities before, during, and after school, recess, physical activity breaks, intramural programs, interscholastic sports, and walking or biking to and from school. Schools play a key role in shaping the social and physical development of their students.

Many know the health-related benefits associated with being physically active, and now the field of exercise science can add brain power to the long list of tried and true benefits. Ratey (2008) refers to the good news as a revolution, so let us take up the cause and raise our heart rates, put our heads together, and pull out all the stops to give children the best chance to be smart, healthy contributing members of society, by providing them with a truly interdisciplinary, holistic education.

Students prefer processing and retrieving information in a variety of ways that educators identify as learning styles. Being informed of Gardner's (1999) theory on Multiple Intelligences enables educators to adjust teaching methods to better serve each individual learner. *Verbal-linguistic* learners use words effectively and have the ability to manipulate the structure or sounds of language. *Naturalistic* learners are good in science, love working outdoors and are especially sensitive to environmental issues. *Interpersonal* learners have the ability to perceive and discriminate between the feelings and moods of others in a variety of interpersonal areas. *Logical-mathematical* learners are sensitive to logical patterns and relationships involving both cause and effect. *Intrapersonal* learners have good self-knowledge and the ability to adapt based on that knowledge. *Visual-spatial* learners are sensitive to color, line, space, shape, form, and the relationships between these elements. *Musical-rhythmic* learners have the ability to perceive and discriminate amongst musical forms and are sensitive to rhythm. *Bodily-kinesthetic* learners use their whole body to express themselves and have specific physical skills such as, coordination, balance, strength and speed. Once educators realize and embrace multiple ways in which students learn, they can effectively reach more students and concentrate on improving both predominant and non-dominant intelligences.

There are five basic human needs according to Glasser's (1965) reality therapy and choice theory (Glasser, 1998). Understanding these needs and the role they play in improved cognition helps to narrow down the broad undertaking of educators. Glasser believes that all behavior is purposeful and motivated by one or more of the following: survival, freedom, belonging, power, and fun. In thinking about the five basic human needs, their common bond is that they can all be met by movement! Survival speaks to fight or flight and survival of the fittest. Freedom suggests that there are no bodily constraints limiting the ability to get up and move. Belonging is the feeling of being a part of something and the ability to feel loved. Power is the strength or control exercised upon the body, in turn, the destiny of the individual. Fun speaks for itself; your first bike ride, running like the wind and dancing! It can be agreed that these are definitely basic human needs embodied by all and these needs plays a major role in human behavior and personality.

Some of the research by Ratey (2008) is so convincing that even opponents of exercise may stand up and take notice. In Naperville, Illinois, a revolutionary before-school fitness program helped to put this school district of 19,000 children, first in the world in science (Ratey, 2008). There are positive relationships between physical activity and modestly improved cognition (California Department of Education, 2002; Dwyer, Sallis, Blizzard, Lazarus, & Dean, 2001). Dwyer et al. (2001) studied Australian children between 7-15 years old and found that across age and sex, academic ratings were significantly correlated with measures of physical activity on specific components of fitness. The California Department of Education, (CDE, 2002) reported a distinct linear correlation between higher levels of physical fitness (students in three grades who met three or more fitness standards) and higher academic performance (Stanford Achievement Test, 9th edition). This research points to the notion that regular physical activity, in particular aerobic exercise, is the best defense for everything from mood disorders to ADHD (attention deficit hyper-activity disorder) to addiction, to menopause, to Alzheimer's disease, and needs to be reframed as benefitting the brain just as much, if not more, than the body (Ratey, 2008)!

The solution begins and ends with the decisions we make. Children are not getting as much physical activity as they should, despite the many benefits. It is important to establish good physical activity habits as early as possible. So how do we do that? By making physical activity and quality physical education a part of your school's culture by increasing the amount of physical activity students participate in, throughout the day, every day. It is critical that we take the steps now to educate and make a change in our student's lives to help them lead a healthier, more productive life. According to the National Association of Sport and Physical Education (NASPE, 2013), physical activity can produce physical, psychological, and social benefits and children who are inactive are more likely to become inactive adults.

Figure 1: "Teaching Strategies for Active Learners: A Framework for Movement for Teachers"

1. ***Preparing the Brain***: There is a connection between a well developed sense of spatial awareness and abstract thinking. The young brain needs to activate this system so movement and cognitive growth can develop (Jensen, 2000). Another key in getting the brain ready to learn is proper hydration, and crossing the mid-line of the body. Cross lateralization games such as, "gotcha" and "interlocking finger find" help develop both sides of the brain; each side of the brain controls the opposite side of the body (Blaydes, 2001). Gilbert's (2000) Brain Dance is composed of eight fundamental movement patterns we are programmed to move through from 0-12 months which wire the central nervous system. The dance uses tactile, visualization, vestibular development and cross lateralization all in one simple, fun activity that is an excellent full body and brain warm-up that can be performed in limited space areas safely. This would be a great addition to the morning announcements to help reorganize the brain and get the body physiologically ready to learn! www.creativedance.org; www.actionbasedlearning.com

2. ***Providing Brain Breaks:*** Shorter is always better. Brain breaks provide necessary content breaks, state management, re-focusing attention, getting up to avoid blood pooling and secretion of melatonin, and incorporating fun and novelty into a lesson. The following are a few examples you can use: Handshake Creation: stand up move around and greet as many people as possible with a new handshake, in the allotted time. Singles Gotcha: Find a partner and face them. Place pointer finger in partners palm and they do the same. On the teachers signal "go", each person simultaneously tries to grab the other person's pointer finger and pull theirs away. Rock Paper Scissors: Partners use this long time game to hone their addition, subtraction and multiplication skills. Instead of shooting rock paper scissors, the partners try to guess the combination of numbers thrown out by each individual (+, x, -). www.davidkatzmd.com The Teachers Manual ABC's for fitness.

3. ***Class Cohesion:*** This serves to build relationship skills, teamwork, and cooperation, with a little friendly competition, when warranted, in a fun environment. Balloon Pop: 2 equal circles joined together by holding hands or interlocking elbows. The object is for the group to keep a balloon in the air and not let go of the person next to them. You may add more than one balloon. Group Juggle: A name learning game that establishes a pattern by always throwing to the same person, (calling their name) and receiving from the same person (thanking them by name), in a circle formation with

the only rule being you cannot throw to the persons on either side of you. The teacher gradually adds more objects and the class is now juggling! mkuczala@thertc.net The Kinesthetic Classroom.

4. ***Support of Physical Activity, Exercise, & Fitness:*** Ratey (2008) gives you all the support you need to promote physical activity, movement, and aerobic exercise, not only in school, but district wide: Aerobic exercise was as effective as antidepressants in one landmark study. The Naperville Illinois fitness program helped put one U.S. school district of 19,000 students first in the world in science. Aerobic exercise sparks new brain-cell growth. Ratey, J.A. Spark: The Revolutionary New Science of Exercise and the Brain.

5. ***Teaching New Content:*** Learning new content and trouble- shooting problem areas in math, science, english and geography, such as the water cycle, language rules, slap counting, and map reading; www. actionbasedlearning.com (Jean Blaydes); Finding the circumference and diameter of a circle, understanding the sugar-insulin-insulin resistance relationship; mkuczala@thertc.net; The Kinesthetic Classroom; www. activityworks.com for grades 1-3; www.movingandlearning.com Leaping into Literacy.

6. ***Reviewing Content:*** A silent review game that involves many different content areas while students get up and move to exchange questions with other students. An active, joyful way to review content. Many educators love the idea of students being active, while on task, and quiet all in one activity. mkuczala@thertc.net.

Chapter 2

How to Get Started?

This chapter will provide a framework that consists of seven phases for schools to follow in order to effectively implement the PASS initiative.

Phase One: The PASS Commitment

Phase one is the most critical, and involves making a commitment to become a physically active school system. The goal is to get everyone on board with imbedding physical activity throughout the school day. Obesity encompasses more than being overweight. It has a more severe and direct effect on one's health. To be obese is to have a body mass index (BMI) at or above the 95th percentile. Falling into this category often creates a negative self image. This in turn has a negative effect on academic achievement as outlined in the following data:

Physical Inactivity (YRBS, 2011 Data): Today's youth are considered the most inactive generation in history, according to the American Obesity Association.

- Two-thirds of Hispanic (61.1%) and black (65.9%), and half (45.3%) of white students, do not get the recommended level of physical activity during an average week.
- One out of every 9 students (11.5%) did not participate in at least 60 minutes of physical activity in the seven days prior to administration of the YRBS survey.

- More than 1 in 4 CT. high school students watches TV for 3 hours or more on an average school day; this rate is highest among black (46.0%) and Hispanic (32.4%) students.

Connecticut Department of Public Health, 2011. Connecticut School health Survey Youth Behavior Component. Hartford, CT, June 2012. http://www.ct.gov/dph/lib/dph/hisr/pdf/cshsresults_2011ybcreport_web.pdf

- Adolescents who are overweight have an estimated 80% chance of being obese as adults; and, if overweight begins before age 8, obesity in adulthood is likely to be more severe.
- An estimated $856 million of adult medical expenditures are attributable to obesity each year in Connecticut.
- Obesity kills more Americans each year than AIDS, cancer and injuries combined. At this rate, the current generation of children will not live as long as their parents.

Finkelstein, EA, et al. 2004. State-level estimates of annual medical expenditures attributable to obesity. Obesity Research 12:18-24.
Shape of the Nation report, 2012 American Alliance of Health, Physical Education, Recreation, and Dance. Connecticut State Profile.

This growing condition produces a critical demand for quality and daily physical activity and physical education throughout the school day. It is necessary that the goal of all educators is to achieve an overall improved community that is conducive to a child's freedom and safety in physical activity for their health, well-being, academic achievement and social acceptance. It should be required that all schools incorporate a minimum of 60 minutes of physical activity (as recommended by the CDC) embedded throughout the school day, every day beyond the allotted time for recess and physical education. Therefore, by making the PASS commitment school systems can begin to work towards achieving this goal. Below are the current state standards for Connecticut, where PASS originated. These vary from state to state, in order to better define your commitment to PASS check your state's standards.

Figure 2 "Connecticut State Standards"

1. **Amount of Required Physical Education:** Connecticut mandates physical education in grades K-8, and high schools must provide physical education courses.
2. **High School Graduation Requirements:** The state requires students to earn 1.0 physical education Credit for graduation.
3. **Substitutions:** Substitution of other activities for physical education credit required for high school Graduation is not permitted.
4. **Exemptions/Waivers:** Students need a physician's written order for a medical exemption from high school physical education credit and this medical exemption requires an appropriate alternative.
5. **Physical Activity:** The state does not require elementary schools to provide daily recess and does not require a minimum weekly amount of physical activity time for elementary school students. Neither does the state require a minimum weekly amount of physical activity time for middle school/junior high school and high school students. Classroom physical activity breaks are not required, but Connecticut does prohibit the use of withholding physical activity, including recess, as punishment for disciplinary reasons, as well as the use of physical activity for inappropriate behavior. Connecticut does support Safe Routes to School programs.
6. **Local School Wellness Policy:** The state requires schools or school districts to provide their local school wellness policy to the state education agency and monitors the implementation of local school wellness policies through school food service program compliance reviews.
7. **State Standards:** The state has developed its own standards for physical education, although school districts are not required to comply. The Healthy and Balanced Living Curriculum Framework for Comprehensive School Health Education and Comprehensive Physical Education was last revised in 2006 and is based on the national standards.
8. **State Curriculum:** The state does not require the use of specific curricula for elementary, middle school/junior high or high school physical education, but allows local school systems and individual schools the option of using a commercial curriculum such as SPARK or CATCH.
9. **Class Size:** The state mandates a teacher-to-student ratio comparable to other curricular areas.
10. **Online Physical Education Courses:** The state does not allow required physical education credits to be earned through online physical education courses.
11. **Student Assessment Requirements:** The state requires student assessment for physical fitness in grades 4, 6, 8 and 10. The data are sent to the state as congregate data for the school and for the district.

12. **Grade Point Average (GPA):** Physical education grades are not required to be included in a student's GPA.
13. **Fitness Assessment:** The state requires school districts/schools to assess students' physical fitness levels using the "Third Generation Connecticut Physical Fitness Assessment."
14. **Body Mass Index (BMI):** The state does not require schools to collect students' BMI or height and weight.
15. **Certification/Licensure of Physical Education Teachers:** The state requires certification or licensure of Physical education teachers at the elementary, middle school/junior high and high school levels. Physical education is taught only by certified physical education teachers. For certification, teachers must earn a score of at least 175 on the "Physical Education Content & Design Test #0095." This certification must be renewed every five years.
16. **Professional Development of Physical Education Teachers:** Professional development, continuing Education hours or credits are required in order to maintain/renew one's physical education teacher certification or licensure. No state funding is provided for this professional development.
17. **Temporary Certification:** Temporary/emergency teacher certification may be granted for less than one year to anyone holding a bachelor's degree in any subject area.
18. **National Board Certification:** The state does not actively encourage physical education teachers to become certified through the National Board Certification process.
19. **District Physical Education Coordinator:** The state does not require each school district to have a licensed physical educator serving as a PE coordinator.

Other Notes: Connecticut is a "local control" state, so in many of these areas, the state has recommendations for local districts and schools rather than requirements.

Contact Person:
Dr. Jean Mee: Jean.Mee@ct.gov
Physical Education & School Health Education Consultant

Phase Two: Identifying PASS Resources

Within phase two it is important to identify all available resources in order to help define

The mission, goals, and action plan for PASS These could include, but are not limited to, supplies, facilities, and equipment, personnel, and funding. First determine what programs currently exist in your school system, i.e., before and after school programs, physical education, intramurals, community programs (YMCA), etc. Second, evaluate these programs in order to determine how extensive, inclusive and effective they are.

- Physical Resources: determine availability of supplies, indoor and outdoor facilities, and equipment that are conducive for effective implementation of physical activity.
- Personnel: determine availability of faculty, staff, administrators, parents, community members, and other volunteers, such as, teacher education students, to help organize and implement physical activity in a variety of settings.
- Funding: determine your financial need and source of funding for the PASS initiative. Funding may be required for supplies, equipment, facilities and personnel, and may vary from year to year depending on your program.

Phase Three: Identifying PASS Stakeholders

Identify and collaborate with all stakeholders, which include but are not limited to, administrators, faculty/staff, students, parents, community members, and all those interested in seeing improvement in the school environment. A crucial piece of phase three is to provide an informational meeting that outline the responsibilities of the various members of the PASS team and are listed below:

PASS Team

- Write a mission statement, goals and objectives for the PASS initiative.
- Evaluate the needs of the school system.
- Develop a PASS action plan.

- Organize and Implement the PASS initiative "Kick-Off"
- Help motivate, maintain, and sustain the PASS initiative.

School Boards

- Provide leadership
- Provide equipment, resources and appropriate facilities
- Provide key stakeholders opportunities for input in the PASS initiative
- Provide staff training
- Provide appropriate funding to support PASS
- Provide administrators, faculty and staff with ongoing support
- Develop partnerships with community organizations
- Become role models for all children
- Understand the benefits of physical activity
- Advocate for the PASS initiative

Administrators

- Commitment to the PASS initiative
- Create a positive and supportive environment for the PASS initiative
- Collaborate with school board, faculty and staff to support the PASS initiative
- Monitor faculty's implementation of the PASS initiative
- Provide support and resources to assist teachers in the implementation of the PASS initiative
- Participate in the PASS initiative
- Communicate with school board, faculty and staff, students, parents and the community
- Provide opportunities for input from school board, faculty and staff, students, parents and the community relating to the PASS initiative
- Become role models for all children
- Understand the benefits of physical activity
- Advocate for the PASS initiative

Faculty & Staff

- Commitment to the PASS initiative

- Monitor and assess the progress of the PASS initiative
- Create a positive and supportive environment for students' involvement in the PASS initiative
- Provide appropriate inclusive activities for all students to implement the PASS initiative
- Provide opportunities for feedback and input from students
- Become role models for all children
- Understand the benefits of physical activity
- Advocate for the PASS initiative

Students

- Commitment to the PASS initiative
- Actively participate in PASS activities
- Become role models at school, home, and in their community
- Identify the benefits of physical activity
- Advocate for the PASS initiative

Parents

- Understand and support the PASS initiative
- Provide input and feedback for the PASS initiative
- Provide opportunities for family involvement in physical activity at home
- Become a role model for their children
- Participate in the PASS initiative
- Advocate for the PASS initiative

Community Partners

- Commitment to support the PASS initiative
- Provide input and feedback regarding the PASS initiative
- Create partnerships with the school board for facility and equipment usage
- Provide appropriate, training, resources and funding for implementation of the PASS initiative
- Alignment of existing organizational goals and/or initiatives with the PASS initiative

The Pass initiative should be structured using the top down and bottom up approach, and facilitated with care, in order to provide stakeholders with the opportunity to connect, communicate, cooperate and collaborate for ultimate success in a physically active school system.

Phase Four: Developing a PASS Needs Assessment:

The purpose of this assessment is to determine where and how much physical activity already occurs in your school and community. This will help you identify the strengths and weaknesses of your current programs involving physical activity and highlight areas of need. The following PASS needs assessment is a sample that can be adjusted for use in your school. (Refer to Figure 3).

- Determine whether the initiative is going to be implemented in one classroom, grade level, or school wide.
- Determine when, where, and how much physical activity will be imbedded within the school system.
- Set a timeline and a kick off date for implementation, ie, opening of school, quarterly, or after a holiday break. The PASS Kick-off: will signify the start of the implementation of a physically active School system
- Determine how long it will take your school system to be fully engaged in PASS

P.A.S.S.			
Needs Assessment			
Opportunities for Implementation	**What physical activities are you doing now?**	**If collaborating, with whom?**	**What would you like to add in the future?**
Before/After School			
During School			
Recess/Lunch			
Physical Education			
Family/Home			
School/Community Events			

For each opportunity for implementation, identify in the box provided what if any physical activity you are currently doing, who you might be working with and what you might want to consider incorporating in the future.

Phase Five: Promotion and Kick-Off of the PASS Initiative

It is important to publicize the PASS initiative through a variety of vehicles. Provide data and research to support the need and benefits of incorporating physical activity throughout the school day. Train the PASS team to be knowledgeable and prepared to field questions from the media regarding the PASS initiative. Some ideas for promoting the initiative are as follows:

- Advocacy Tool Kit: provided on the Society of Health and Physical Educators website. www.shapeamerica.org
- Social Media: use local T.V and radio networks, Facebook and twitter to get the word out about the PASS initiative and Kick Off event
- Newsletter: send information home monthly updating parents and community members on the PASS initiative
- District & School Websites: create websites that educate community members on the benefits of PASS

- Student, Teacher & Parent Testimonials: highlight the achievements of students, such as increases in standardized academic and fitness test scores, to the media, board of education, etc.
- rewards and incentives among stake holders for participation, such as certificates and diplomas
- promotional materials that build excitement such as t-shirts, flyers, buttons, hats, pins, wrist bands, etc.
- PASS Kick-Off Event: Outline a plan for the event, such as a school-wide field day, assembly, community walk, pep rally etc. and then set the date. Invite all key stakeholders and a local celebrity to attend the event. Make sure some element of the Kick Off includes 1-2 minute brain breaks /energizers at the beginning middle and end of the event. Include hands on, inclusive stations that promote the PASS initiative.

Phase Six: Implementing and Maintaining PASS:

Implementation

All key stakeholders need to make the important connection between the brain and the body. Physical activity during school reinforces the link between classroom curriculum and movement. I t facilitates retention, concentration and positive behavioral attributes. There are three types of physical activity that can be imbedded throughout the school day.

- The first is, content rich activities that directly links curriculum to movement, and anchors learning.
- Brain breaks, that might include, cross lateralization and rhythmic activities, can help stimulate the brain and prepare it for learning; an excellent example of this is The Brain Dance (Gilbert, 2000).
- The final type of physical activities are just plain fun, they don't necessarily link to curriculum, but help students to refocus, reengage, and reinvigorate their desire to learn.

For a complete listing of all the resources to get your PASS initiative started refer to Chapter 9.

Family and community support should play a critical role in getting children and adolescents participating in physical activity beyond the school day. They can act as positive role models by engaging in physical activity themselves to promote lifelong physical activity in their children.

- Families should try to incorporate physical activities into their daily routines and engage in local school and community physically active events.
- Communities should provide a variety of opportunities for their members to be physically active, and should work with schools to increase and promote physical activity engagement.
- Collaborate with other local organizations to promote and host events that advocate for a physically active community. Examples might include family fun runs, health & wellness fairs, and active transport. See Chapter 9.

Schools and communities can provide a variety of strategies and approaches to help students become more physically active, that include quality physical education programs and opportunities that increases access to physical activity for all students to be physically active not just during physical education class but throughout the day. Students can get most of their physical activity through a quality physical education program that is complemented by activities.

- Before, during, and after school, physical activities
- Intramural & interscholastic sport programs
- Walking or biking to and from school
- Participating in community and family based physical activities.

Maintaining:

The key to any successful program is sustainability. The action plan of the PASS initiative should include a variety of ways that the school system can maintain the program so it doesn't become yet another passing "fad". Some examples could include but are not limited to the following:

- Administer on-going evaluation throughout the initiative for modification, adjustment and success.
- The importance of daily physical activity needs to be reinforced on all levels in order to be successful.
- Use faculty/staff, parents, community members to keep the PASS initiative vital.
- Follow-up discussions need to occur with all the key stakeholders regarding progress of the PASS initiative.
- Create PASS initiative "boosts" throughout the school year.
- On-going development of new physical activity ideas to reinvigorate the PASS. initiative.
- Provide on-going professional development for faculty & staff as needed.
- Provide information about opportunities for students, parents, and guardians to participate in physical activities throughout the summer months, such as, open gym night, physical activity packets, fitness fairs, summer physical activity journal, community based activities, etc.
- Promote local summer programs that involve physical activity such as, camps, YMCA, parks and recreation, biking and walking trails, town pools, etc.

Chapter 3

Before and After School Activities

This chapter will provide several ideas and resources for before and after school activities. Children need to start their day off with the right mind set. Physical activity helps to prepare the brain for learning by providing a healthier body and mind that work more effectively. Movement improves brain function and should be part of every child's before and after school routine, along with a healthy breakfast and a good night's rest.

Schools can increase students' physical activity levels by incorporating more movement into out-of-school time programs. The National Afterschool Association (NAA) recommends that at least 30 minutes of before or after school program time should be devoted to physical activity with a focus on both muscular strength and cardiovascular activities. Before and after school physical activity programs provide opportunities for all students to engage in safe, supervised activities, develop social interaction skills and reinforce what they've learned in physical education while working towards the nationally recommended 60+ minutes of daily moderate-vigorous physical activity. Schools can increase students' opportunities to participate in daily at-school physical activity by incorporating more movement into out-of-school time programs, through intramural activities, interscholastic sports and other before and after school programs. Additionally, before and after school activities provide staff, parents and other community members with a variety of ways to get involved in the development of their students' health and well-being.

As part of PASS, incorporating a before and after school program can be a powerful tool for increasing physical activity, reducing obesity, and providing students with an opportunity to develop healthy habits. Schools play a critical role in helping children lead active, healthy lives. Physical education, recess, and before and after-school programs, all have the potential to get kids moving. Research shows that kids who are physically active aren't just healthier, they tend to have improved cognition, increased focus and attention and behave better in school. Unfortunately, schools do not offer enough opportunities for children to be active and many are even cutting existing programs.

Before and after school programs have the power to make daily physical activity accessible and engaging for every student and to help all students discover and instill the love of lifelong movement. The goal of these programs is to create high-quality physical activity programs that expand and enrich the learning opportunities of the regular school day.

Providing high-quality before and after school programs is a collaborative process. When implementing before and after school programs, as part of PASS collaboration may occur with staff, parents and students as well as community and other local organizations. Forming before and after school partnerships to implement and evaluate quality programs will help provide support, funding and resources.

Before and after school staff and/or volunteers can play a critical role in helping students develop the necessary skills and knowledge to lead an active and healthy lifestyle. Teacher to student ratio is important when developing before and after school programs as part of PASS The organization, structure and positive interaction that these adults can provide will help students feel relaxed and confident when participating in physical activities. Collaboration with community partnerships can also assist in providing additional staff members and volunteers. Proper adult supervision of these programs will ensure that all activities are safe, appropriate and fun for all. Liability concerns can create obstacles when implementing before and after school programs as part of

PASS However, developing a partnership between schools and local organizations can help address and overcome some of these barriers. Shared liability can be of added value for schools and community partnerships when providing programs.

When implementing PASS before and after school activity programs, the National physical education standards provide an outline of the skills and knowledge that students need to stay active throughout their lives and should be used as a framework for incorporating essential skills into the program. An important benefit to physical activity is that it can take on many different forms and the activities can vary greatly. When planning activities it is important to carefully consider the purpose of each activity as well as the needs, interests, and ability levels of the students involved. Research suggests that participation in a wide variety of physical activity can provide significant benefits to a person's physical, cognitive, motor, social, emotional, and educational development. PASS before and after school activities need to be developmentally appropriate, organized and should provide clearly articulated goals and objectives. Students should be allowed the opportunity to choose activities that best meet their needs and interests.

Before and after school programs may be the best opportunity to engage students in physical activity that would otherwise not be available to them. The following are guidelines and samples of activities for incorporating before and after school programs into PASS.

Physical Activity Before and After School
A summary from NASPE/AAHPERD on before and after school activities:

Opportunities include:
- Walk and bike to school and implementation of a comprehensive Safe Routes to School program
- Informal recreation or play on school grounds
- Physical activity in school-based child-care
- Physical activity clubs and intramural sports
- Interscholastic sports

White House Task Force on Childhood Obesity Report to the President

- State and local education agencies should be encouraged to provide opportunities in and outside of school for students at increased risk for physical inactivity, including children with disabilities, children with asthma and other chronic diseases, and girls.
- Federal, state, and local educational agencies, in partnership with communities and businesses, should work to support programs to extend the school day, including afterschool programs, which offer and enhance physical activity opportunities in their programs.
- State and local education agencies should be encouraged to support interscholastic sports and help decrease prohibitive costs of sports by curbing practices such as "pay-to-play," working with other public and private sector partners.
- The Federal Safe Routes to School Program (SRTS) should be continued and enhanced to accommodate the growing interest in implementing Safe Routes to Schools plans in communities.
- The Environmental Protection Agency should assist school districts that may be interested in siting guidelines for new schools that consider the promotion of physical activity, including whether students will be able to walk or bike to school.
- "Active transport" should be encouraged between homes, schools, and community destinations for afterschool activities, including to and from parks, libraries, transit, bus stops, and recreation centers.
- Local governments should be encouraged to enter into joint use agreements to increase children's access to community sites for indoor and outdoor recreation.

ACTIVITY IDEAS:

1. **Finding Fitness Fun Day:** Green Street School (K–6, 262 students) in Brattleboro, Vermont developed an innovative

way to increase physical activity in the school community while raising funds for class trips, the winter sports program and a school community garden. The school implemented a month-long program encouraging students to engage in active play or moderate movement for a minimum of twenty minutes prior to school at least two days per week. Students went to the community—friends, family, neighbors—to get monetary sponsorship for their activity and raised over $20,000 through this activity-based program. The event culminated in a celebratory *Finding Fitness Fun Day*. See Additional Vermont Examples: Physical Activity/Physical Education for more.

2. **Move to Learn Lab (Blaydes, Wallingford, CT):** Movement to Learn labs like the ones in Wallingford Ct. provide before school opportunities for students to prepare the brain for learning. It is a motor development program based on brain research which supports how movement improves brain function. Based heavily on Jean Blaydes Madigan's Action Based Learning, the lab is a series of progressions and stations that are designed to get the brain ready for input and processing. The activities consist of rolls, creeps and crawls, spins, twirls, bounces, balances, walks, jumps, juggles and supports his/her own weight in space while developing sensory components of balance, coordination, spatial awareness, directionality and visual literacy, The activities can be varied depending on age and need, and changed periodically throughout the school year. Levels of fitness are increased and academic concepts are reinforced. As students move from station to station with their group, they experience better self-awareness, self-esteem and improved social skills.

3. **Activity Promotion Laboratory:** The Activity Promotion Laboratory at East Carolina University College of Health and Human Services. The goal of the Activity Promotion Laboratory is to promote active lifestyles. The document includes a Healthy Active Children Resource Sheet and tips for Creating a Physically Active Classroom Atmosphere. Energizers are designed for K-5.

Some activities include: Heart Smart, Stop, Drop and Roll or Rescue 9-1-1. Energizers are available for a free PDF format download at: Download at East Carolina University- Activity Promotion Laboratory.

4. **Walk and Bike to School**: Start a walking club before or after school. Invite parents to participate, track miles and reward efforts. Organize a **National Walk** or **Bike to School Day**: National Walk to School Day is held in October and Bike to School Day is held in May.

5. **Think, Pair, Share, Fitness Walk:** Upon arrival students, faculty and staff gather together at a designated point (i.e., front entrance, playground, etc) to engage in a school wide 10 minute fitness walk (on school grounds). Each day a topic of discussion will be provided to think about and share with a partner while walking. Upon completion of the activity students will return to classroom and reflect on the topic of the day, through a formal writing activity, such as journaling. Inclement weather- walk will occur indoors.

6. **Walking School Bus or Bicycle Train:** Students walk or ride their bikes to school with adults serving as "bus drivers." Have families take turns walking their kids to school or develop a more formal, structured route with meeting points, a timetable and a rotating schedule of trained volunteers.

7. **Safe Routes to School (SRTS):** Run by the Federal Department of Transportation, SRTS has resources, activities and funding to make walking and biking to school safe and routine in your community.

8. **Walking or Running Club:** Make it simple – ask the principal, a teacher or other adult to lead students on a regular morning walk or run, or check out some of these established programs to bring to your school:

   - New York Road Runners Mighty Milers: www.nyrr.org/youth-and-schools/mighty-milers

- Girls on the Run: www.girlsontherun.org/
- orldFit: www.worldfit.org/

9. **After School Drop in Physical Activity:** An organized before or after school drop in physical activity session where faculty, staff, parents and students will be given an opportunity to participate in various physical activities, throughout the school year, such as, yoga, fitness activities, zumba, walk/run, and organized games.

10. **HOP'N, After-School Project:** Designed to prevent obesity through a quality after-school program. The HOP'N After-School Project includes four elements: a daily healthy snack, daily physical activity, weekly nutrition and physical activity education sessions. Eight elementary schools participated in an after-school program in Lawrence, Kansas where children wore pedometer devices to measure their physical activity.

11. **WORLDWIDE DAY OF PLAY EVENT:** Hosting a Worldwide Day of Play event is fun and totally doable! The event can be big, small, an hour long, or all day. Worldwide Day of Play is a great way to increase visibility around your organization's commitment to physical activity, sports, and recreational activities. Kids just need to have fun and get the message that **Play is important!** This guide provides tips to help you plan an event for your organization. Be sure to register your event at **nickbighelp.com/public/register-wwdop-event.php** to gain access to exclusive planning resources.

12. **GIRLS ON THE RUN:** Girls on the Run is a transformational physical-activity-based, positive youth development program for girls in grades 3 to 8. The organization teaches life skills through dynamic, interactive lessons and running games. The program culminates with participants being physically and emotionally prepared to complete a celebratory 5k running event. Throughout the season, girls develop and improve **competence,** feel **confidence** in who they are, develop strength of **character,**

respond to others and oneself with **care and compassion,** create positive **connections** with peers and adults, and make a meaningful **contribution** to community and society.

13. **Intramural sports:** Intramural programs provide students with a variety of fun interesting and challenging activities that meet the needs and interest of all students. The primary focus is on the enjoyment of learning and not on competition or winning. Additionally students develop positive attitudes, increase self-esteem, enjoy positive social interactions, and increase their overall health and fitness levels.

14. **Interscholastic Sports:** Designed to promote the physical, mental, social, and emotional well-being of the individual players. It provides opportunities to participate in physical activity that will increase strength, skill, coordination, overall health and fitness. Additionally students learn about responsibility, sportsmanship, pride, school spirit, and fair play.

Resources

Action for Healthy Kids – http://www.actionforhealthykids.org

This website provides resources and information about nutrition and health-related activities in Pennsylvania and other states across the U.S.

Amateur Sports for Kids - http://www.amateur-sports.com/kids.htm

List of 10 exercises and jumping activities with directions to complete exercise, and body area or muscle group exercised.

American Alliance for Health, Physical Education, Recreation and Dance -

http://www.aahperd.org/index.cfm

The American Alliance for Health, Physical Education, Recreation and Dance (AAHPERD) is the largest organization of professionals supporting and assisting those involved in physical education, leisure, fitness, dance, health promotion, and education and all specialties related to achieving a healthy lifestyle.

Centers for Disease Control and Prevention Guidelines for School and Community Programs to Promote Lifelong Physical Activity among Young People -

ftp://ftp.cdc.gov/pub/Publications/mmwr/rr/rr4606.pdf   These guidelines identify strategies most likely to be effective in helping young people adopt and maintain a physically active lifestyle. The guidelines were developed by CDC in collaboration with experts from other federal agencies, state agencies, universities, national organizations, and professional associations

Centers for Disease Control and Prevention: Health Topics – Physical Activity http://www.cdc.gov/HealthyYouth/physicalactivity/brochures/index.htm

Parent, teacher, and Principal brochures about providing physical activity for children

Centers for Disease Control and Prevention: Physical Activity Evaluation Handbook

http://www.cdc.gov/nccdphp/dnpa/physical/handbook/pdf/handbook.pdf

This handbook outlines the six basic steps of program evaluation and illustrates each step with physical activity program examples.

Centers for Disease Control and Prevention: Promoting Better Health for Young People

Through Physical Activity and Sports

http://www.cdc.gov/HealthyYouth/physicalactivity/promoting_health/pdfs/ppar.pdf

This report outlines ten strategies to promote health and reduce obesity through lifelong participation in enjoyable and safe physical activity and sports.

Functional Fitness 4 Kids, Inc. - http://www.ff4k.org/

This non-profit organization was created to combat the current youth obesity epidemic, address the need for quality after-school activities, and teach strategies and skills necessary to live a healthy lifestyle.

International Life Sciences Institute. Take 10! - http://www.take10.net

This is a classroom-based physical activity program for students in Kindergarten through 5th grade.

Kids Health - http://www.kidshealth.org/index.html

KidsHealth provides doctor-approved health information about children from before birth through adolescence. Created by The Nemours Foundation's Center for Children's Health Media, this site provides families with accurate, up-to-date, health information.

National Association for Sport and Physical Education - http://www.aahperd.org/naspe/

NASPE is a non-profit professional membership association that sets the standard for practice in physical education and sports. Its 16,000 members include K-12 physical education teachers, coaches, athletic directors, athletic trainers, sport management professionals, researchers, and college/university faculty who prepare physical activity professionals.

Pennsylvania Advocates for Nutrition and Activity, PANA - http://www.panaonline.org

PANA's website includes information about a variety of programs and special events that promote nutrition and physical activity.

Project PA, Promising Practices: Ideas, Advice, and Models for Successful Local Wellness

Policy Implementation -

http://nutrition.psu.edu/projectpa/promisingpractices/PDF/PromisingPractices.pdf

PA During and After School Day 8 February 2008. This is a collection of "Promising Practices" related to local wellness policy implementation from Pennsylvania schools.

Web walking - http://walking.about.com/cs/measure/a/webwalkingusa.htm

Plan activities for lessons in geography, math, health, science and reading as you "travel" across the United States

Chapter 4

During School Activities

The Center for Disease Control, CDC, recommends that children and adolescents participate in at least 60 minutes of light to moderate physical activity on all or most days of the week and students need access to physical activity throughout the day to even come close to meeting these recommendations (USDHHS, 2008). Students are more likely to participate in activities that appeal to them and are developmentally appropriate. Many and varied options for physical activity should be available to students. One of the ways schools can achieve this goal is by adhering to the PASS guidelines for physical activity during the school day, which include but are not limited to, content rich activities, brain breaks, energizers, hallway activities for between classes and breaking for lunch and recess. A minimum of one 5-10 minute physical activity (PA) break should be included within each one hour teaching block. An example of what this might look like is provided in Table 1. Please note that this table can and should be modified to fit your school's schedule and needs.

Including physical activity during the school day helps students focus on positive behavior and interactions with others, builds self-confidence and self-efficacy, and is one of the things that help in the development of lifelong habits of exercise and physical activity. It also provides opportunities for students to practice what they have learned in physical education, prepares the brain for learning, and to ultimately work toward the nationally recommended 60 minutes of physical activity per day (USDHHS, 2008). By infusing physical activity into classroom lessons the educator provides yet another opportunity to include meaningful activities that anchor learning, improve time-on-task behaviors, decrease absenteeism, and increase daily in-school physical activity levels among children. Educators will now have the potential to positively influence children's behaviors and lifetime choices by including physical activity, and at the same time, maximize student learning during academic activities that are otherwise sedentary.

Recess, in most American schools, consists of a 15-30 minute period usually following or as part of the lunch period. During recess students should have freedom to choose what they want to do and with whom. This having been said, some school districts might want to hire a qualified person or utilize the physical educator to construct and implement planned recess periods on several days of the week.

This chapter will provide samples of content rich activities, brain breaks, and energizers connected to the Common Core State Standards in math and language arts where applicable, and provided for you in the PASS lesson plan template. (See Appendix A for blank lesson template).

Table 1

PASS: During the School Day					
8:30-8:50	School wide PASS walk				
8:50-9:00	School wide Physical Activity - Brain Dance (Led by student morning announcer)				
Classroom Schedule					
Time	Language Arts	Math	Social Studies	Science	Special Areas
9:00-10:00	Teaching Block				
9:50-10:00	PA Break				
10:00-10:50		Teaching Block			
10:50-11:00	PA Break				
11:00-11:50					Teaching Block
11:50-12:00	PA Break				
12:00-1:00	Lunch and Recess: Structured and un-structured physical activities				
1:00-1:50			Teaching Block		
1:50-2:00	PA Break				
2:00-2:50				Teaching Block	
2:50-3:00	PA Break				
3:00-3:10	School wide Physical Activity – Cool down				

*** Schedule should be modified to meet your
school day timeframe and needs***

LANGUAGE ARTS ACTIVITIES

PASS Lesson Template

Name of Activity: *Syllables and Sentences on the Move*

Safety: *Open personal space*	**Time:** *10-15 minutes*

Facility: *All* ❒ Classroom ❒ Multipurpose ❒ Gymnasium ❒ Outdoors	**Equipment:** *None*

Physical Activity Level: *Light* ❒ Light ❒ Moderate ❒ Vigorous	**Type of Activity:** *Content Rich (LA)* ❒ Brain Break/Energizer ❒ Content Rich ❒ Fun

Common Core Connection: *L.3.1i*
Syllables and sentence structure

Activity Description:
Syllables & Sentences on the Move
- Small groups of 3-4
- Clap out syllables in Name and/or simple Sentence
- Create a movement that coincides with the number of syllables in name/sentence
- State Name/sentence and the number of syllables and then perform motion as you speak
  Variation: in a circle students can learn names by mimicking everyone's movements to their name. Let students create simple sentences to put movement to and eventually they could work together as a class and create a paragraph dance.
  Aids memory, speaking and listening skills, and producing simple sentences.
  For Example: The flowers are pretty (six syllables)

Grade Level Modifications: *Use grade level appropriate subject related words, spelling words or sight words to create sentences*

PASS Lesson Template

Safety: *Create 4 clear pathways to front of room (between rows of desk)*	**Time:** *10 minutes*
Facility: *All* ☐ Classroom ☐ Multipurpose ☐ Gymnasium ☐ Outdoors	**Equipment:** *Alphabet flashcards, lettered tennis balls or other small items that can be lettered*
Physical Activity Level: *Moderate* ☐ Light ☐ Moderate ☐ Vigorous	**Type of Activity:** *Content Rich (LA)* ☐ Brain Break/Energizer ☐ Content Rich ☐ Fun

Common Core Connection: *L.3.2e*
Spelling

Activity Description:
Words with Friends
- 4 teams traveling between desks to front of room
- 4 buckets, one per team in the front of the room. Have minimum of 2 sets of the alphabet in each bucket
- On command, 1 member at a time goes to their bucket and takes 1 letter back to team, each member goes and continues to collect letters until they are able to form a word
  Variation: can create own word or use spelling/vocabulary words and can give a minimum number of letters each word must have.

Grade Level Modifications: *Use grade level appropriate subject related words, spelling/vocabulary words or sight words*

PASS Lesson Template

Safety: *Open Personal Space*	**Time:** *10 minutes*
Facility: *All* ❒ Classroom ❒ Multipurpose ❒ Gymnasium ❒ Outdoors	**Equipment:** *None*
Physical Activity Level: *Moderate* ❒ Light ❒ Moderate ❒ Vigorous	**Type of Activity:** *Content Rich (LA)* ❒ Brain Break/Energizer ❒ Content Rich ❒ Fun

Common Core Connection: *L.3.1e*
Verbs and adverbs

Activity Description:
"As If"
- Run in place as if a big scary bear is chasing you
- Walk forward as if you are walking through thick chocolate pudding
- Jump in place as if you are popcorn popping
- Reach up as if grabbing balloons out of the air
- Move your feet as if ice skating
- Shake as if you are a wet dog.
  Variation: Note cards with verbs and adverbs, ie hop quickly
  Children Pair up and act out the sentences.

Grade Level Modifications: *Utilize verbs and adverbs that are grade level appropriate*

PASS Lesson Template

Name of Activity: *Beach Ball Buds*

Safety: *Clear Open Space*	**Time:** *10 minutes*
Facility: *All* ❏ Classroom ❏ Multipurpose ❏ Gymnasium ❏ Outdoors	**Equipment:** *1 Beach Ball*
Physical Activity Level: *Light* ❏ Light ❏ Moderate ❏ Vigorous	**Type of Activity:** *Content Rich (LA)* ❏ Brain Break/Energizer ❏ Content Rich ❏ Fun

Common Core Connection: *SL.3.1d*
Communication Skills

Activity Description:
Beach Ball Buds
• Pairs or small groups
• In a circle, have students toss beach ball with questions on it back and forth
• Questions can include the following:
  ➢ Sometimes I pretend to be…
  ➢ My favorite game is…
  ➢ I am most happy when…
  ➢ I worry about…
  ➢ I am interested in…

Grade Level Modifications: *Create questions that are appropriate to grade level ability*

MATH ACTIVITIES

PASS Lesson Template

Name of Activity: *Math at your Feet*

Safety: *Open Personal Space*	**Time:** *10 minutes*

Facility: *All* 　❏ Classroom　❏ Multipurpose 　❏ Gymnasium　❏ Outdoors	**Equipment:** *None*

Physical Activity Level: *Light* 　❏ Light　❏ Moderate　❏ Vigorous	**Type of Activity:** *Content Rich (Math)* 　❏ Brain Break/Energizer　❏ Content Rich 　❏ Fun

Common Core Connection: *Content.3.MD.C.6*
Measurement

Activity Description:

Math at our Feet

- Teacher calls out various measurements and students follow directions and measure the distance out using the following body parts:
- Toes=Inches
- Foot size=Feet
- Giant Step=Yard

Grade Level Modifications: *Give grade level appropriate distances for measuring*

PASS Lesson Template

Safety: *Personal Space*	**Time:** *10-15 minutes*

Facility: *Classroom*
- ❐ Classroom ❐ Multipurpose
- ❐ Gymnasium ❐ Outdoors

Equipment: *Fruit Loops and bowls/cups*

Physical Activity Level: *Moderate*
- ❐ Light ❐ Moderate ❐ Vigorous

Type of Activity: *Content Rich (Math)*
- ❐ Brain Break/Energizer ❐ Content Rich
- ❐ Fun

Common Core Connection: *3.MD*
Estimation

Activity Description:

Fruity Math
- Teacher gives out fruit loops
- Students estimates # of fruit loops
- Student counts to check estimation and then categorizes loops in groups of 5's or 10's
- Each color represents a movement: Purple= free, Blue= jump, Orange= hop, Green= stretch, Yellow= twist

Grade Level Modifications: *Use grade level appropriate number of fruit loops and multiples*

PASS Lesson Template

Name of Activity: *Operation Catch*

Safety: *Clear Open Space*	**Time:** *10 Minutes*

Facility: *All*
   ❐ Classroom   ❐ Multipurpose
      ❐ Gymnasium   ❐ Outdoors
	Equipment: *Ball or Bean Bag*

Physical Activity Level: *Light*
   ❐ Light ❐ Moderate ❐ Vigorous
	Type of Activity: *Content Rich (Math)*
	  ❐ Brain Break/Energizer ❐ Content Rich
	             ❐ Fun

Common Core Connection: *Content.3.OA.D.8*
Mathematical Operations

Activity Description:
Operation Catch
• Select Partners
• Each pair has a bean bag or ball
• Student 1: says # on throw and the operation (+, -, X or division)
• Student 2: says # on catch and equals = on throw
• Student 1: says answer on catch

Grade Level Modifications: *Use grade level appropriate operations*

PASS Lesson Template

Safety: *Clear Open Space*	**Time:** *10 minutes*

Facility: *All* ☐ Classroom ☐ Multipurpose ☐ Gymnasium ☐ Outdoors	**Equipment:** *None*

Physical Activity Level: *Moderate* ☐ Light ☐ Moderate ☐ Vigorous	**Type of Activity:** *Content Rich (Math)* ☐ Brain Break/Energizer ☐ Content Rich ☐ Fun

Common Core Connection: *Content.3.OA.D.8*
Mathematical Operations

Activity Description:
Fidget Digits
• Select partners
• Teacher calls which operation will be used (addition, subtraction, multiplication or division)
• Using fingers, throw out a number of fingers on one hand
• The first one to solve the equation gets to choose the movement for the pair to perform, the number of times of equation answer
• Example: 3 + 5 = 8 (8 hops on right foot)
• Variation: Students move to find new partner

Grade Level Modifications: *Use grade level appropriate operations & equations*

SOCIAL STUDIES ACTIVITIES

PASS Lesson Template

Name of Activity: *Due North*

Safety: *Open Personal Space*	**Time:** *10 minutes*

Facility: *All* 　　❏ Classroom　❏ Multipurpose 　　❏ Gymnasium　❏ Outdoors	**Equipment:** *None*

Physical Activity Level: *Light* 　　❏ Light　❏ Moderate　❏ Vigorous	**Type of Activity:** *Content Rich (SS)* 　　❏ Brain Break/Energizer　❏ Content Rich 　　　　　　　　❏ Fun

Common Core Connection: *NA*

Activity Description:

Due North

- Place compass points around the classroom
- Students stand next to desk
- Teacher calls out various "directions" i.e., South, North West
- Students quickly face in the proper direction
- If they miss they must return to NORTH and try again

　Variations: Have students move using various movements determined by the teacher, i.e., Go south 4 steps and jump to east, then side step to west.

　Let students call out directions, call out states or towns relative to your location.

Grade Level Modifications: *Use developmentally appropriate movements and/or have upper grade level students use a compass*

PASS Lesson Template

Safety: *Clear Open Space*	**Time:** *10 minutes*

Facility: *All*
- ❐ Classroom   ❐ Multipurpose
- ❐ Gymnasium   ❐ Outdoors

Equipment: *Map of the United States*

Physical Activity Level: *Light*
- ❐ Light   ❐ Moderate   ❐ Vigorous

Type of Activity: *Content Rich(SS)*
- ❐ Brain Break/Energizer   ❐ Content Rich
- ❐ Fun

Common Core Connection: *NA*

Activity Description:

State Body Puzzle
- Assign each student a state
- Students must arrange themselves the way the states appear on a map
  Variations: State capitol or other fact about the state. Large Groups, multiple states, smaller groups use regions/specific landmarks. Could also be done with countries/continents

Grade Level Modifications:

PASS Lesson Template

Safety: *Clear Open Space*	**Time:** *10 Minutes*

Facility: *All*
- ❏ Classroom ❏ Multipurpose
- ❏ Gymnasium ❏ Outdoors

Equipment: *Index cards*

Physical Activity Level: *Light*
- ❏ Light ❏ Moderate ❏ Vigorous

Type of Activity: *Content Rich (SS)*
- ❏ Brain Break/Energizer ❏ Content Rich
- ❏ Fun

Common Core Connection: *NA*

Activity Description:

State Move & Match
- Students are each given a card with either a state or capitol written on it
- On teachers command, students match the states & capitols
- Complete process 2-3 times so students have multiple match opportunities
  Variations: Can also be done with countries and continents, with words and definitions, and with numbers and equations.

Grade Level Modifications: *Use grade level Q & Q/facts about states*

PASS Lesson Template

Safety: *Clear Open Space*	**Time:** *10 minutes*

Facility: *All*
- ❒ Classroom ❒ Multipurpose
- ❒ Gymnasium ❒ Outdoors

Equipment: *None*

Physical Activity Level: *Moderate*
- ❒ Light ❒ Moderate ❒ Vigorous

Type of Activity: *Content Rich (SS)*
- ❒ Brain Break/Energize ❒ Content Rich
- ❒ Fun

Common Core Connection: *NA*

Activity Description:

Virtual State Tour
- Teacher creates a virtual tour of the state
- Students stand by desk and act out the tour

Example: Virtual Tour of Connecticut
- Go for a swim in the Long Island Sound
- Hike the Blue Trail
- Climb up Roaring Brook Falls
- March across the Pearl Harbor Memorial Bridge
- Kayak around the Thimble Islands
- Climb an apple tree at Lyman Orchards
- Throw a TD pass at the Yale Bowl
- Make a jump shot with the UCONN Huskies
- Ski down Mount Southington
- Twirl & toss some pizza dough on Wooster St. in New Haven
- Ride the oldest working Carousel at Bushnell Park

Grade Level Modifications: Add directions (N, E, S, W) to the movements, have students come up with their favorite places and activities and create a "virtual summer vacation"

Change virtual tour to reflect states or countries studied at specific grade level

SCIENCE ACTIVITIES

PASS Lesson Template

Safety: Open Personal Space	**Time:** *10 minutes*

Facility: *All*
    ❐ Classroom   ❐ Multipurpose
    ❐ Gymnasium   ❐ Outdoors
	Equipment: *None*

Physical Activity Level: *Light*
    ❐ Light   ❐ Moderate   ❐ Vigorous
	Type of Activity: *Content Rich (Science)*
	    ❐ Brain Break/Energizer ❐ Content Rich
	                  ❐ Fun

Common Core Connection: *NA*

Activity Description:

Active Weather
- Use current day forecast or seasonal forecast (spring, summer, winter, fall)
- Stomp for thunder
- Clap for Lightening
- Tip toe like the clouds
- Swing/sway like the wind
- Shiver for the cold
- Collapse in the heat

Grade Level Modifications: Use developmentally appropriate movements to challenge students. Use grade level appropriate words to depict weather patterns/forecast

PASS Lesson Template

Safety: *Open Personal Space*	**Time:** *10 minutes*
Facility: *All* ❑ Classroom ❑ Multipurpose ❑ Gymnasium ❑ Outdoors	**Equipment**: *CD Player & Instrumental music for The Hokey Pokey*
Physical Activity Level: *Light* ❑ Light ❑ Moderate ❑ Vigorous	**Type of Activity:** *Content Rich (Science)* ❑ Brain Break/Energizer ❑ Content Rich ❑ Fun

Common Core Connection: *NA*

Activity Description:
Funny Bones (Done to the tune of the Hokey Pokey)
- Use anatomical terms instead of the ones in the song
- Identify bones of body: Humerus, ulna, fibula & tibia, patella, ribs, pelvis, carpals, cranium, sternum tarsal, phalanges and femur.
- Example: "You put your tarsals in, you put your tarsals out, you put your tarsals in and you do the body shake, you do the body shake and you turn yourself around, that's what it's all about.
Variations: Could use the major muscle groups of body

Grade Level Modifications: *Identify body parts/muscles that are appropriate to grade level.*

PASS Lesson Template

Safety: *Open Personal Space*	**Time:** *10 minutes*
Facility: *All* ☐ Classroom ☐ Multipurpose ☐ Gymnasium ☐ Outdoors	**Equipment:** *None*
Physical Activity Level: *Moderate* ☐ Light ☐ Moderate ☐ Vigorous	**Type of** *Activity: Content Rich (Science)* ☐ Brain Break/Energizer ☐ Content Rich ☐ Fun

Common Core Connection: *NA*

Activity Description:

Rise and Fall of the Heart

- Teacher discusses where the heart is located=Left side of chest
- What is the size=Fist
- Function=Delivers blood and nutrients to the body
- What helps strengthen the heart=exercise
- What weakens the heart=smoking, overweight, unhealthy habits
- When students hear "weakening activities" they fall to the ground

Examples: eating a Big Mac, smoking, no fruits and vegetables, watching T.V.

- When students hear "strengthening activities" they jump up

Examples: dancing, walking the dog, riding a bike, participates in PASS

Grade Level Modifications: *Use grade level appropriate facts/activities about what strengthen and weakens the heart*

PASS Lesson Template

Safety: *Clear Open Space*	**Time:** *10 minutes*

Facility: *All*
  ❑ Classroom ❑ Multipurpose
  ❑ Gymnasium ❑ Outdoors
	Equipment: *Labeled Posters*

Physical Activity Level: *Moderate*
  ❑ Light ❑ Moderate ❑ Vigorous
	Type of Activity: *Content Rich (Science)*
	  ❑ Brain Break/Energizer ❑ Content Rich
	❑ Fun

Common Core Connection: *NA*

Activity Description: Jump Start your Heart
• Teacher labels poster board with the 6 parts pertaining to the heart:
  Example: Rt. Atrium=jogging
  Rt. Ventricle=shadow boxing
  Lft. Atrium=jump rope
  Lft Ventricle=twisting
  Lungs=X country skiing
  Body=chop wood
• Students are divided into 6 groups and are at each part of the heart, located around the room
• Teacher calls out "start your Heart"
• Students perform the movement at their labeled station
• Teacher calls out "blood flow"
• Students move to the next appropriate part of the heart or station, and perform the new movement there.

Grade Level Modifications: *Use grade level labels for various part of the heart. Use developmentally appropriate locomotor movements*

BRAIN BREAK/ENERGIZER ACTIVITIES

PASS Lesson Template

Name of Activity: *"Gotcha"*

Safety: *Clear Open Space*	**Time:** *10 Minutes*

Facility: *All*
    ❒ Classroom ❒ Multipurpose
    ❒ Gymnasium ❒ Outdoors
	Equipment: *None*

Physical Activity Level: *Light*
    ❒ Light ❒ Moderate ❒ Vigorous
	Type of Activity: *Brain Break/Energizer*
	  ❒ Brain Break/Energizer ❒ Content Rich
	               ❒ Fun

Common Core Connection: *NA*

Activity Description:

"Gotcha" is a Brain break that also utilizes cross lateralization
- Students are in pairs or in one large circle
- Right hands are held out palm up and left hand index finger is placed in partners, right palm or in the palm of the student next to them

    Variation: in a circle the students can cross their arms and do the same thing, so circle needs to move in and get smaller.

Grade Level Modifications: *Increase or decrease the speed of calling "Gotcha".*

PASS Lesson Template

Safety: *Clear Open Space*	**Time:** *10 minutes*
Facility: *All* ❏ Classroom ❏ Multipurpose ❏ Gymnasium ❏ Outdoors	**Equipment:** *None*
Physical Activity Level: *Light* ❏ Light ❏ Moderate ❏ Vigorous	**Type of Activity:** *Brain Break/Energizer* ❏ Brain Break/Energizer ❏ Content Rich ❏ Fun

Common Core Connection: *NA*

Activity Description:

"Toe Tapping" is a fun energizer
- Stand up and find a partner
- Face partner
- Tap Right foot – RT Foot 1X (Count out loud)
- Tap Left foot – LFT Foot 3X (Count out loud)
- Tap Right foot – RT Foot 2X (Count out loud)
- Continue 1, 3, 2 pattern how fast can you go?

Grade Level Modifications: *Select developmentally appropriate movement patterns.*

PASS Lesson Template

Safety: *Clear Open Space*	Time: *10 minutes*
Facility: *All* ❑ Classroom ❑ Multipurpose ❑ Gymnasium ❑ Outdoors	Equipment: **1 Hula Hoop**
Physical Activity Level: *Light* ❑ Light ❑ Moderate ❑ Vigorous	Type of Activity: *Brain Break/Energizer* ❑ Brain Break/Energizer ❑ Content Rich ❑ Fun

Common Core Connection: *NA*

Activity Description:
"Helium Hoop" is a class cohesion brain teaser
- 8-10 students are gathered around a large hula hoop
- Students hold the hoop by placing it on their outstretched index fingers (palms facing)
- As a team the student try to lower the hoop to the ground
- No one's fingers can come off the hoop, if this happens the group has to start again
- Hint: inevitably the hoop rises, ergo the name "helium" hoop.

Grade Level Modifications: *Adjust the height of starting point and/or position of body. (start seating, kneeling or on feet)*

PASS Lesson Template

Safety: *Clear Open Space*	Time: *10 minutes*
Facility: *Light* ❒ Classroom ❒ Multipurpose ❒ Gymnasium ❒ Outdoors	Equipment: *None*
Physical Activity Level: *Light* ❒ Light ❒ Moderate ❒ Vigorous	Type of Activity: *Brain Break/Energizer* ❒ Brain Break/Energizer ❒ Content Rich ❒ Fun

Common Core Connection: *NA*

Activity Description:
"Loop Da Hoop" is a class cohesion brain break
- Students get into groups of 5 with one hula hoop per group
- Students join hands and move hoop around circle without breaking hands

Grade Level Modifications: Adjusting the size of the group or adding a second hoop moving in opposite directions.

PASS Lesson Template

Safety: *Open Personal Space*	**Time:** *10 Minutes*
Facility: *All* ❏ Classroom ❏ Multipurpose ❏ Gymnasium ❏ Outdoors	**Equipment: None**
Physical Activity Level: *Moderate* ❏ Light ❏ Moderate ❏ Vigorous	**Type of Activity:** *Brain Break/Energizer* ❏ Brain Break/Energizer ❏ Content Rich ❏ Fun

Common Core Connection: *NA*

Activity Description:

"Brain Dance" By Anne Gilbert is brain energizer

• Deep Breathing (3X)

• Tactile Pressure: Create a body pattern that will be repeated with each of the following movements:

    1. Squeezing (using your hand to squeeze your body in the sequence you have designed).

    2. Light tapping

    3. Brushing

       Purpose to stimulate blood flow

• X an O is a full body stretch Repeat each 2X

       Purpose is to stretch all parts of body

• Raindrop is a head to toe stretch of the spinal column. Pretend that a drop of rain has landed on your head and you are rolling it down spinal column to toes and back up.

       Purpose is lengthwise stretch

• Follow your Hands and Arm: Stretch one arm out to side and keeping it straight move it across the front of your body to the other side. Be sure you are visually tracking the moving arm and the upper body remains square to the hips. (Do Not Move Shoulders)

       Purpose is visual tracking skills and increase midline crossing

• Puppet Stretch: on same side of body reach up with your arm and leg (4X)

       Purpose to increase unilateral coordination, balance

• Climbing Stretch: reaching up with opposite arm and leg (4X)

       Purpose to increase bilateral coordination, balance

• Cross Over: Touch opposite elbow to knee and repeat (4X)

       Purpose to increase midline crossing, bilateral coordination and balance

• Spinning: This a very important part of dance, spin till dizzy in one direction and stop and right yourself, and then do the same in the opposite direction

       Purpose to create vestibular stimulation and increase muscle tone, to teach the body to right itself, to learn to listen to body signals.

Grade Level Modifications:

In conclusion, choosing creative activities for children is a healthy way to help them grow and learn. A child is engaged on a creative level every time he/she draws paints, builds with blocks, plays games, reads and engages in a variety of other activities. By providing PASS, and adding physical activity to the school day the educator is helping to develop imagination, problem solving skills, teamwork, and to build both gross and fine motor skills,

Chapter 5

Recess

Recess for elementary school students can be structured or unstructured. Unstructured recess or "free play" is an important component of PASS and play with peers could include hopscotch, tag, kickball and jump rope. Recess also functions successfully as an established school-based activity and should be carefully considered as part of any school health and wellness policy. Children have limited opportunities to interact with other children in an unstructured environment while at school. Experts agree that free play is just as vital as academic time to a child's educational, social, and emotional development. Despite the evidence that children need an outlet in order to "blow off steam", and learn how to interact with others, all while getting much needed exercise, nearly 40 percent of American elementary schools have either eliminated or are considering eliminating recess due to school budget cuts, increased focus on academic standards and teacher evaluations.

Studies have shown that kids who are given the opportunity to take a break from their hectic academic schedules actually develop and perform better than those who go without, and as such the National Association for Sport and Physical Education (NASPE) has released the following position statement concerning recess:

"All elementary school children should be provided with at least one daily period of recess of at least 20 minutes in length. Recess is an essential component of a comprehensive school physical activity program and of the total education experience for elementary school students. Various organizations including the United States Department of Health and Human Services and the United States Department of Education (USDHHS & USDE, 2000), Centers for Disease Control andPrevention (CDC, 1997), National Association for the Education of Young Children (NAEYC, 1998), and American Association for the Child's Right to Play (IPA/USA, n.d.) support school recess as an integral component of a child's physical, social, and academic development. Recess provides children with discretionary time to engage in physical activity that helps them develop healthy bodies and enjoyment of movement. It also allows children the opportunity to practice life skills such as cooperation, taking turns, following rules, sharing, communication, negotiation, problem solving, and conflict resolution. Furthermore, participation in physical activity may improve attention, focus, behavior, and learning in the classroom (California Department of Education, 2005; Hannaford, 1995; Jarrett, 1998; Jensen, 2000; Shephard, 1997; Symons, Cinelli, James, & Groff, 1997). Currently 16 percent of our nation's children are overweight as a result of poor nutritional habits and a lack of physical activity (Hedley, et al., 2004). An increasing number of children are developing cardiovascular risk factors (e.g., high blood pressure) and type 2 diabetes (Kaufman, 2002). Daily physical activity is an important part of the solution to these health issues. National recommendations state that school-aged children and youth should participate in at least 60 minutes per day of moderate to vigorous physical activity (NASPE, 2004; Strong, et al., 2005; USDHHS & USDA, 2005). Participation in a regularly scheduled recess period can make an important contribution toward meeting this recommendation. In addition, extended periods of inactivity (two hours or more) are discouraged for elementary-age children." (NASPE, 2004)

The playground is an essential part of any school and every community. Children spend many hours of their day occupying themselves with what the playground has to offer. The nearby neighborhood may enjoy both its appearance and it could function as a fitness park for the community. The following are some of our favorite recess activities complete with resources:

Outdoor/Indoor Recess Activities:

1. **Tag games**, such as Heads & Tails, Blob Tag and Pairs Tag are non elimination tag games that allow students to have fun while working on their cardiovascular efficiency.

2. **Four Square** is easy to setup with simple rules and contributes to eye-hand coordination. Mark off four squares on the playground and label each one with a sheet of paper, 1, 2, 3, and 4. Write the same numbers on small slips of paper and place in a cup. Tell the children to run around the squares until you shout, "Four squares." When you yell this, each child must select a square and stand in it. After the children each select a square, draw a slip of paper from the cup. If you draw the number 2, all children standing in square number 2 are out of the game. Tell the children to select another number and draw again. If you draw a number and no children are in the square, draw again. Keep playing until only one player remains in the game, and she is the winner.

3. **Jump Rope** activities such as Turn style, Double Dutch, Long and Short Rope activities provide cardiovascular benefits for students.

4. **Hop Scotch** works on coordination, balance, take-off and landing, and patterning.

5. **Kick the Can** place a can, such as an empty coffee can, in the middle of the play area. Select one student to be "it" first. The "it" player must stand by the can and count to 30, while the other players run and hide. After "it" counts, he will walk or run around to try to find the other players. If "it" spots a player, that player must run and kick the can in order to be safe. If "it" tags the player before he kicks the can, he is the new "it" for the next game

6. **Find the Flag** divide the children into two teams and give each team a small cloth. Use a rope to divide the playground in half

and have each team get on opposite sides. When you say, "Go," the teams must hide the cloths. After both Teams hide the cloths, they must switch sides. The first team to find the "flag" wins the game.

7. **Roaring Lion** select one child to be the "roaring lion" and have her sit with her back to all the children. Place a small lion cub plush toy behind the "roaring lion." When you say, "Go," the children must try to sneak up on the roaring lion and take her lion cub. If the lion hears someone sneaking up, she can roar and turn around to look. If she catches someone moving, that player is the new roaring lion. Any player who successfully reaches the lion cub wins the game.

   http://www.ehow.com/info_8002712_playground-games-schools.html#ixzz2gyMf8ygc

8. **Jam a Minute School Program** – Health-E-Tips. The goal of the Health-E-Tips program is to help kids make an impact on combating childhood obesity. The website requires that you sign up. The JAM School Program brings physical activity and health education into the classroom. JAM is designed to teach kids (and adults) healthier lifestyle habits. JAM is a free wellness resource for schools. JAM resources offer a weekly one-minute exercise routine called JAMmin' Minute, an athlete-featured more extensive routine called JAM Blast, and a monthly health newsletter called Health-E-tips. According to the website the program can be led by a JAM leader or student appointed "Drill Sergeant" of the week and could be done at recess!

9. **Indoor Recess Games** – Proteacher. This website has a number of indoor games for recess. Proteacher identifies these activities as "fun ideas for what to do when recess is in the classroom." Indoor games can be printed out from the website. They are free resources. Each game idea is an open thread where other teachers write in to add their game ideas and game modifications.

10. **Peaceful Playgrounds 2 Go Games – Peaceful Playgrounds** is a great resource for parents, educators and school administrators. – Darell

Hammond, CEO, KaBOOM! – Huffington Post. www. peacfulplaygrounds.com.Peaceful Playgrounds 2 Go Game rugs are available for purchase and allow you to take some of the more popular outdoor games and markings indoors. Six game rugs are currently available including: Alphabet Grid, Number Grid, Hopscotch, Balance Beam, Bean Bag Toss, and Target. All games include a number of academic activities that go with the movement activities.

11. **Ten Activities to Encourage Physical Activity in the Classroom** – Therapy Source. 10 easily implemented activities that can be conducted during an indoor recess. Activities listed on the board and various students are assigned to lead each activity. Activities include: Walking Worksheets, Opposite Hunt, and Pencil Jumps.

12. **A Range of Breaks to Use in the Classroom** – Behavior Solutions. Ideas such as Sitting Aerobics, Finger Aerobics, and Double Doodles/Palm to Palm. Modified activities from Dave Vizard Brain Breaks, Starter Activities and Fillers.

13. **Fitness Fun Forever** – Florida Department of State. This website is unique in that it lists great games for getting kids moving. Some games like Balloon Frantic is an indoor classroom game that is popular with students. The site has a listing of games, followed by a video clip of the teacher explaining the game, as well as a video clip of students performing the activity in addition to a downloadable description card. Download game description cards and view videos:

14. **Take 10!** – International Life Science Institute. Take 10 is a classroom-based physical activity program for K-5. The tool was created by teachers for teachers and students. It integrates academic learning objectives with movement. It requires no special equipment and comes with 30 multi-level activity cards linked to reproducible worksheets and was designed to allow students to be active within space limitations of a standard-size classroom.

15. **Hand games** - Remember the old clapping games and songs? The following You Tube Website has about 14 different Hand

clap games and songs. Teaching a game every couple of days can keep students busy trying to perfect the routine and engaged both physically and cognitively. Some favorites include: A Sailor, Dr. Pepper, Miss Mary Mack, and Double, Double. http://www.youtube.com/watch?v=Swe99oRW4wY

16. The **We Count Walking Program** uses pedometers as an aid to kids in fighting fat. The complete program kit ensures your success with the **We Count!** Walking Program. Each set includes 12 Student pedometers, 1 Teacher pedometer, progress charts, certificates, logs, newsletters and motivational stickers. The program's design is based on research that indicates that inexpensive step-counting devices (pedometers) motivate and educate kids to walk and be more active, thereby impacting the alarming number of overweight children. This innovative new program is designed to get kids fit with the slogan, **"Get Fit, Don't Sit"**.

17. **MARBLES from** www.Spark.org 1 playground ball per student Create a large (30X30 paces) activity area. Pair students; identify Player 1 and Player 2.Give each student a ball. Scatter partners throughout the activity area, facing each other 5 paces apart. The object is to kick your ball so it taps your partner's ball. To do that, Player 1 steps behind the ball, allowing Player 2 to make a kick (or roll) to try and tap it Player 2 makes their 1 kick. If the ball hits Player 1's ball, great! If not, Player 1 will pass it back and Player 2 gets 2 more chances. After 3 attempts, players switch roles. Challenges: How many times can you hit your partner's ball before Recess ends? Move back 1 giant step after you hit your partner's ball 3X. The game is best played on grass where balls don't roll too far/fast.

18. **Play Fitness:** Create 15-20 fitness stations around the playground so students can address the 5 health related components of fitness (Body Composition, Cardiovascular, Muscular Strength, Muscular Endurance, and Flexibility) and the 6 skill related components of fitness (Agility, Balance, Coordination, Speed, Power, and Reaction Time).

Chapter 6

Family and Community Activities

Getting parents and community involved in activities outside of the school day is a key component of PASS Research shows that participation in physical activity is influenced by participation and support of parents and siblings. Families that play together spend more time together and experience certain health benefits. Families can support PASS by joining in evening and weekend events and serving as volunteers. Community involvement allows the use of school and community resources such as facilities and personnel, and creates collaboration between school-based and community-based physical activity opportunities.

Family and community programs should provide access to a variety of facilities that support a variety of physical activity. Facilities may include classrooms, multipurpose rooms, playgrounds, fields, parks and other community facilities. Additionally, they should have a designated area where staff can safely implement planned programs and physical activities. Facilities used by families and communities must be accessible to all, including those with disabilities or other special needs. Facility use is one of the most effective ways to meet the needs of the families and community members that participate in physical activity programs. Securing proper facilities is often a collaborative process that involves cooperation among community partnerships that may share space, resources, and/or facilities. These collaborative partnerships allows all participants in PASS regardless of their race, socio-economic status or other limitations to have full access to all facilities that will promote healthy, active lifestyles. Forming community partnerships can help ensure that students have safe and easy access to all community and family programs. Proper equipment is also necessary to ensure the success of all before and after school physical activity programs. Equipment supports students' development and the reinforcement of physical activity skills that they can be used in school, after school and in everyday life.

The Physical educator can work in conjunction with classroom teachers and administrators to organize and advertise events that involve both parents and community members. Planning projects with Community organizations such as the YMCA, Parks and Recreation departments, Faith based organizations, Boys and Girls clubs, Community centers, and Fitness centers and allows for collaboration among many varied stakeholders involved with the success of PASS In addition, the American Alliance of Health, Physical Education, Recreation, and Dance suggest aligning family and community activities with the following National Public Health Campaigns:

National Physical Activity Plan

- Provide access to and opportunities for high-quality, comprehensive physical activity programs, anchored by physical education, in Pre-kindergarten through grade 12 educational settings. Ensure that the programs are physically active, inclusive, safe, and developmentally and culturally appropriate.
- Develop and implement state and school district policies requiring school accountability for the quality and quantity of physical education and physical activity programs.
- Provide access to and opportunities for physical activity before and after school.
- Expand "Safe Routes" initiatives at national, state, county and local levels to enable safe walking and biking routes to a variety of destinations, especially to schools.
- Develop partnerships with other sectors for the purpose of linking youth with physical activity opportunities in schools and communities.

- Promote programs and facilities where people work, learn, live, play and worship (i.e., workplace public, private, and non-profit recreational sites) to provide easy access to safe and affordable physical activity opportunities.
- Provide access to and opportunities for physical activity before and after school.

White House Task Force on Childhood Obesity Report to the President

- Federal, state, and local educational agencies, in partnership with communities and businesses, should work to support programs to extend the school day, including afterschool programs, which offer and enhance physical activity opportunities in their programs.
- "Active transport" should be encouraged between homes, schools, and community destinations including to and from parks, libraries, transit, bus stops, and recreation centers.
- Increase the number of safe and accessible parks and playgrounds, particularly in underserved and low-income communities.
- Local governments should be encouraged to enter into joint use agreements to increase children's access to community sites for indoor and outdoor recreation.
- The business sectors should be encouraged to consider which resources, such as fields and gyms can be used in increase students' access to recreational venues. Corporations, for example, may have large grounds that they can make available for children in the community to play soccer or engage in other activities.

Healthy People 2020 Objectives

- Increase the proportion of the Nation's schools that provide access to their physical activity spaces and facilities for all persons outside of normal school hours, including weekends, summer and other vacations.

- Increase the proportion of adolescents who meet current Federal physical activity guidelines for aerobic physical activity and for muscle-strengthening activity.
- Reduce the proportion of adults who engage in no leisure-time physical activity
- Increase the proportion of adults that meet current Federal physical activity guidelines for aerobic physical activity and for muscle strength training.

The following is a list of expert organizations, agencies and websites provided by www.Aahperd.org:
- National Association for Sport and Physical Education
- Action for Healthy Kids
- National PTA – Physical Activity
- ASCD – Healthy School Communities
- Boys and Girls Clubs of America
- Catholic Youth Association
- JCC Association
- National Council of Youth Sports
- National Recreation and Park Association
- The Y
- National Coalition for Parent Involvement in Education
- BlazeSports America

Practical Resources
- Healthy School Report Card
- Play On! Playground Learning Activities for Youth Fitness
- Opening School Grounds to the Community After Hours: A Toolkit for Increasing Physical Activity Through Joint Use
- Joint Use Resources
- California Project LEAN – Joint Use of School Facilities
- KaBOOM! Playspace Finder – Community Mapping Tool
- KaBOOM! Project Planner – Build & Renovate Playspaces

- Guidelines for Participation in Youth Sport Programs: Specialization Versus Multiple-Sport Participation
- Choosing the Right Sport and Physical Activity Program for Your Child
- Energy Balance 101
- America On the Move
- Physical Activity Kit: Staying on the Active Path in Native Communities

According to author Richard Louv, today's children have become disconnected from nature, or as he likes to put it, are suffering from "nature deficit disorder." Instead of spending endless hours outside riding bikes and climbing tress i.e. being kids, they are playing video games, surfing the web, watching TV and texting. Connecticut's State Parks and Forests offer opportunities for children to fully disengage from technology and go outside and PLAY through the *No Child Left Inside*˙ initiative We welcome you to take the *No Child Left Inside*˙ pledge:

I pledge to defend the right of all children and every family to play in a safe outdoor environment. I will encourage and support opportunities for them to exercise their right by:

- Splashing in clean water and breathing clean air
- Digging and planting seeds in healthy soil and watching what grows
- Climbing a tree and rolling down a grassy hill
- Skipping a stone across a pond and learning to swim
- Following a trail and camping under the stars
- Catching a fish, listening to songbirds and watching an eagle in flight
- Discovering wildlife in their backyard
- Soaking in the beauty of a sunrise and sunset
- Finding a sense of place and wonder in this ecosystem we call Earth
- Becoming part of the next generation of environmental stewards.

Photos from Family Fishing Day - Osbornedale State Park, Derby

Seining

Fishing at Picketts Pond

Fishing at Picketts Pond

Fishing at Picketts Pond

CARE Instructors Who Made the Day Possible!

Great Fishing Day!

Ready to Fish!

Fresh Catch!

Catch of the Day!

Photos from Family Boating Day
- Bigelow Hollow State Park, Union

Boating Safety Bingo

Cold Water Submersion

Canoeing

Flare Demonstrations

Kayaking

Practice Makes Perfect!

Trying Out the BUI Goggles

Trying Out the BUI Goggles

Family Picnicking Day
- Harkness Memorial State Park, Waterford CT.

Horseshoes

Lawn Golf

Garden Themed Picnic

Island Themed Picnic

Parachute

Croquet

Lawn Bowling

Sac Races

No Child Left Inside is a registered trademark of the CT Department of Energy and Environmental Protection

Enjoy hosting these special family physical activity events in the evening and outside of school hours where the whole school is invited. These activities would be organized by the Physical Educator to promote the benefits of physical activity outstide of the school day.

1. **Family Activity Night** - provide a special evening for families with a monthly theme. Potential activities can be seasonal in focus, instruct families in activities available in the community (climbing, hiking, biking), or provide fitness activities that can be enjoyed by multiple age groups together.

2. **Special Running Events** - consider a special running-themed event each month that allow for friendly participation by family members of all ages, such as a Halloween Fun Run, Turkey Trot, or Reindeer Dash.

3. **Fabulous Fitness Fun** - schedule an evening where families come together and circulate through stations that teach them about health-related fitness, and introduce them to strategies for incorporating activity throughout the day. Families would come to the gymnasium and participate in physical fitness activities based on the five components of health related fitness, which the students are tested on in grades 4, 6, 8, and 10 throughout the year. The Physical Educator can also provide families with simple physical activities that support or enhance the learning of academic content areas as well as the skills and knowledge to become physically educated and advocates for the PASS initiative. Great for all grade levels, this activity can provide targeted learning opportunities for families. Secondary students already familiar with health-related fitness can focus on skills for an active lifestyle. Prepare fitness stations that focus on the skill-related fitness components that older youth can choose for an active lifestyle, and invite representatives from local venues to provide some introductory activities.

4. **School Dance Night** - present a night of dancing through the decades and provide a variety of popular, line, social, and

freestyle dances that are used throughout the lifespan. Every age group is guaranteed to have a great time! Introduce a variety of dances and music that represent the many cultures of your school community.

5. **Wellness Fair** - at all grade levels, both parents and student will appreciate an evening designed for learning about the unique wellness needs of busy families. Incorporate wholistic activities that focus on the multiple dimensions of wellness.

6. **Bicycle Safety Rodeo** - collaborate with local representatives from the Department of Transportation, law enforcement, and bicycle advocacy groups to present a bicycle safety rodeo. Focus on basic safety skills for elementary school students, and for secondary students, change it up to concentrate on commuter skills for active transportation safety.

7. **Family Yoga Night** - provide an activity night that focuses on the benefits of yoga for stress reduction, balance, and flexibility.

8. **Community Fitness Fair** - invite local health clubs to your middle or high school to share what they have to offer youth as they become independent fitness consumers.

9. **Parks and Recreation Night** - invite your local Parks and Recreation Department to present sample activities that are offered in your local program-a great way to introduce families to their many free to low-cost activity options.

10. **Collaboration Stations** - present an activity night that focuses on collaborative activities that can be participated in with partners, trios, and small groups and focus on collaborating with others

Chapter 7

Excerpts from the Field

PASS can be seen in a variety of ways depending on the district needs, type of students, levels of comfort by faculty, interest, and motivation. The level of implementation can also vary from a small scale, starting with one class or grade level and eventually encompassing the whole school system. Spreading the good news about the PASS initiative

Best Practices:

Berlin, CT. McGee Middle School
- Incorporate the classroom curriculum throughout the Physical Education curriculum on a regular basis.
- Utilize study hall periods to embed physical activity
- Host Parent "climb" nights, activities in conjunction with March Madness, and a walking club called the McGee Milers
- Were on "COOL SCHOOLS" in CT.

Burlington, CT. Region 10
Coordinator for Physical Education and School Health Education provides these examples:
- 2 teachers are piloting the physical activity in the classroom initiative. A second grade teacher is doing energizers several times a day. She incorporates high energy exercises with accompanying music as well as yoga poses with relaxing music. We put together a packet of activities that were used during

the year and our plan is to present this project in August and get some other teachers to participate. We'll have the booklet of activities that have been tested and were successful along with a starter kit of beanbags, scarves and hacky sacks for the volunteer teachers.

- A high school math teacher is incorporating energizers sporadically in 2 of her classes-not every period, but at least 1 day/week.

Glastonbury, CT. Hebron Avenue School Grade Level: K-4

How do you actively bring the classroom curriculum into the gymnasium?

- Social studies: integrate study of culture in various countries for each grade level by introducing games from those countries; integrate games Native Americans played for 4th grade social studies unit on regions; integrated games from countries 1st grade classes were introduced to in their study of celebrations around the world; 1st grade and 2nd grade classes used maps of the playscape to move from place to place;

- Language arts: students created a poem from a tumbling routine they created in PE; in small groups, 4th grade students created exercise posters for some of the components of physical fitness – flexibility, muscular endurance and muscular strength using photography and word processing skills; 1st grade students created "What Am I" riddles after using the parachute; 4th graders wrote stories with "hints for preparing for the physical fitness tests" for incoming 4th graders;

- Math: create maps and special score cards for score keeping for Frisbee golf, soccer golf etc. or any other opportunity; complete pedometer worksheets to add steps and create graphs of the results; math facts tag games to reinforce math facts in addition, subtraction and multiplication; when creating jump rope routines in 4th grade, use patterns of 4's and 8's with a total of 32 to 48 beats;

How do you bring physical activity into the classroom(s)?

- When the gymnasium and outdoor facilities are unavailable, you can conduct PE classes in the classroom. Classroom teachers can observe how physical activity can be handled in the space.
- Create special programs to encourage classroom teachers to give activity breaks to students – Winter Walks – 3 maps for indoor walking trails were created for teachers. Outdoor trail and various themes were used to create interest and reinforce academic learning.
- Provide workshops during professional development time or informally when speaking with classroom teachers to give ideas for infusing physical activity into classroom activities. Suggest books, internet resources etc. to assist in the process.

How do you advocate for your PE program with parents, and/or in the community in general?

- Create a display for parents to see when participating in Open House activities.
- Involve parent volunteers in JRFH events.
- Involve parent volunteers in Sport and Fitness Festivals.
- Write an article for every school newsletter about what is happening in Physical Education.
- Send home physical activity calendars periodically throughout the school year and summer.
- Serve on PTO committees; volunteer at PTO events.
- Send photos to the local newspaper highlighting special events or regular class activity.
- Post informative, colorful bulletin boards in the hallway and keep them updated.
- Write Mini Grants to develop programs which will enhance instruction and allow the purchase of special equipment for the school – pedometers. Publicize receipt of the grants.
- Post information for the school community on the school website.

Fairfield, CT. Riverfield School Grade Level: K-5

How do you actively bring the classroom curriculum into the gymnasium?

- I frequently use their word wall words, units of instruction and areas of CMT's we are low. Map Runs delve into geography, estimation and spelling. Alphabet warm-ups literacy, I use TONS of Math.

How do you bring physical activity into the classroom(s)?

- I've done workshops for my classroom teachers to provide them with ideas. I do one idea/activity at each faculty meeting to keep ideas on the fore front and provide more ideas.
- I email teachers frequently and tell them how they can help enhance PE topics such as telling teachers we just finished the fitness test, have your students write out it, How To's for writing…have them write how to do a jump rope trick…etc.

How do you advocate for your PE program with parents, and/or in the community in general?

- I have a web page that I keep up to date
- I use a PE newsletter a few times a year that goes to all families informing them of what we are doing in PE
- I'm involved in many different school extracurricular activities so I'm "out there" with the parents constantly talking about the program (Running Club, Jump Rope for Heart, PTA events)
- I inform the newspapers when I have a big program going on.

Fairfield, CT. McKinley Elementary School

We try to infuse PE classes with the academic curriculum as much as possible. Some examples are as follows:

- When the 5th grade students were having trouble with pronoun identification, I created a card game to be used in a relay race. Students ran out to grab a card and determined if it was a pronoun or not. If it was a pronoun s/he brought it back to the starting spot. There, the group either verified it was a pronoun or not and at times a discussion was needed by the team to make a final decision.

- Spelling words for the 2nd graders as well as 5th graders have been used in a scooter activity where students had to ride to find letters their teams needed.

- Math skills are always used in tallying scores and dividing students into teams. Counting by 5s and 10's with K and 1st grades are practiced with regularity.

- Science and health terms are the focus of units (like basketball) where force, friction, levers, identifying bones, muscles and basic anatomy are incorporated.

- Nutrition is visited several times a year in PE and at each grade introducing concepts and themes at age appropriate levels. A food pyramid activity that identifies the number of fat grams a food has is a favorite of 4th graders.

- We have a student run morning video telecast of McKinley News and we have a minute of physical activity demonstrated by a 4th or 5th grader on the broadcast. Students in their classrooms follow along and perform the minute of activity.

- Classroom teachers have brain buster activities that are physical and pull from them when the children are transitioning or after sitting for an extended period of time. Some teachers take a walk around the outside of the school building and after 10 laps the students receive a "foot token" to add to their chain.

- We write in the school newsletter a section titled "Footnotes from the Gym". In this bimonthly newsletter we review some of the skills and units we have recently covered; we introduce the upcoming units, brag about some of the children's achievements (Biggest Winner) and remind parents of the importance of good nutrition, wearing proper footwear and clothing as well as have links to pertinent websites.

- If we have an event that merits an article and photographs in the local paper, we provide them ourselves.

- We have a dedicated PE bulletin board and at times plaster the halls with photos from current units to share with parent visitors (especially during parent-teacher conferences).

Hamden, CT. Bear Path & West Woods Elementary Schools

- ABCs for Fitness is being implemented in 3rd grade classrooms at Bear Path Elementary and West Woods Elementary Schools.

Hartford, CT. Maria Sanchez Elementary School

- We have instituted a classroom-based activity program for grades K-4 called "Activity Works" http://www.activityworks. com/activityworks.php.
- I think it's a fabulous program. Here is their description: Activity Works is a classroom-based program that uses 10-minute guided audio and video adventures to combine physical activity and cognitive learning, engaging bodies and minds to develop healthy behaviors and renew focus. Each activity segment incorporates age-appropriate exercise and movement, validated by experts for safety and effectiveness. It is designed for classroom teachers to take 10-12 minutes during anytime of the day that best meets their needs and take their class through a scripted exercise journey. There are 20 short little vignettes, 15 of which are audio on CD's and five others that are video segments.
- Activity Works is a simple media program that combines standards-based kinetic learning and cardio fitness in a 12-minute classroom experience for grades 1 through 3. Research-based trials in Long Island schools demonstrated academic and physical benefits to children who participated in the Activity Works program.
- Our teachers seem to like it and seem to use it to varying degrees. We have also made it part of our physical education classes on occasion. I would love to have this reporter come to my school to check it out. You would be more than welcome as well. I am attaching the link to their site if you need or want more info.

Meriden, CT. Hanover Elementary School
- Reinforces vocabulary words and math concepts throughout the Physical Education curriculum
- Introduced Brain Dance to 3rd graders and plans to teach it to all additional grade levels
- Sent home a packet to parents of their students doing the Brain Dance with their teachers

Portland, CT.

After her brother, a member of the PE Cadre of Trainers in CT, talked her ear off about the connection between moving and learning, a high school English teacher in Portland, CT. decided to incorporate it into her classes. She has lessons that both involve moving (she created a small-side team relay involving questions/answers from a reading passage) along with lessons that have movement and brain breaks. Not only does she enjoy it, but the students do, too. Since the lesson was so unique and successful, she invited administrators to come observe.

Southington, CT: Hatton Elementary School

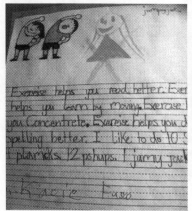 

A second grade class was having difficulty passing a geography test on direction. The Physical Educator replicated the map and the test and made it into a game in PE. Students were retested with a 100% pass rate. This activity precipitated collaboration with classroom teachers to create more games like this in the PE setting. Additionally the district began to train teachers and implement physical activity in the classroom through a pilot program at the 2nd grade level. Due to the success of this program they are now in the process of expanding the program throughout the elementary schools. This school district continues to strive to become physically active, with the Superintendent and Assistant Superintendent collaborating with the YMCA to provide training in PASS.

Physically Active Classroom Earns Grant

March 21, 2013
By Ed Harris
Editor – Southington Observer

Schools in Southington will get a little more active thanks to a grant from Anthem Blue Cross and Blue Shield. The insurance company bestowed the school system with a $24,000 grant that will be used to help combat childhood obesity through the Physically Active Classrooms program. The program is a collaboration between the Southington school systems, the YMCA and Bradley Hospital. "It truly is an epidemic in this country," Anthem Blue Cross and Blue Shield VP of Sales Jim Augur said about childhood obesity. "We need to figure out ways to keep kids active." Augur said the Physically Active Classroom program will do its part to keep kids active. Dave Donnelly, a grant writer for the YMCA that helped secures the grant. The grant money will be used to help teach the teachers and staff how to utilize the programs and implement it throughout the district. The program has attracted attention in Hartford, with Southington state Senator Joe Markley jumping on board and showing his support. Southington School Supt. Dr. Joseph Erardi is very supportive of the program and said it was a good way to a healthy activity in a classroom setting. He said the staff at Hatton was very supportive of the program and that it flowed into the lesson plans, causing no distractions. "It's a huge win, win," Erardi said. "It's hard to find anything on the downside of it." The plan was to use the grant money to integrate the program throughout the district within the next three years.

Miss Connecticut, Sen. Markley and Teachers Get Moving!

Cross Lateralization activity was led by Dr. Marybeth Fede and Carol Ciotto also in the photo Marcia Phelps, physical education teacher, Sen. Joe Markley and Miss Connecticut Emily Audibert.

We are fighting Childhood Obesity

A workshop entitled, Connect – Communicate – Cooperate – Collaborate was held in the cafeteria. Dr. Marybeth Fede of Southern Connecticut State University (SCSU) and Carol Ciotto of Central Connecticut State University (CCSU) put this initiative together with the goal of making all Connecticut schools physically active school systems. During the day long course teachers from kindergarten to fifth grade learned about active classroom activities and how to best bring the idea into their daily curriculum.

Senator Joe Markley added, "A healthy body equals a healthy mind –and good health is a benefit to our whole society."

Hatton Elementary School is the pilot location for the active classroom in this district. In an effort to help kids stay healthy the active classrooms would replace the traditional lesson plan of sitting and listening with active participation. Teachers will connect learning and motion in an effort to get the kids to move.

Miss Connecticut, Emily Audibert from Wolcott has chosen to utilize her title to champion the fight against childhood obesity. "One in three children in America is overweight or obese; this is a dangerous epidemic that is in desperate need of attention and help," said Miss Connecticut, Emily Audibert.

One English teacher experimented with using teams in her classroom. Each team had to act out words on a card to show the difference between adverbs and verbs. The teacher said spelling and math are the easiest subjects to showcase movement in a lesson plan.

In Southington teachers hope to further the active classroom to a point where the traditional desk and chairs will be replaced with adjustable podiums that allow students to stand, or sit on big exercise balls.

Senator Markley would like to see the idea of active classrooms catch on. It's a terrific program that all Connecticut children could benefit from," said Sen. Markley.

Wallingford, CT: EC Stevens Elementary School

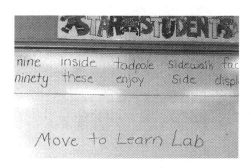

- This district has received grants and implemented action based learning labs (Blaydes, 2000) called Movement to Learn labs in all 8 of their elementary schools. Both the physical educators and the classroom teachers are utilizing the lab to reinforce curriculum and anchor learning.
- The PASS team has just recently (May, 2013) collaborated with the PE teachers in this district to offer assistance in the labs, by providing PETE students to do their internships in the labs. This is a win-win situation for everyone involved, PASS gets data from the labs, Wallingford PE teachers get much needed help running the lab, and future PE teachers from CCSU, and SCSU get valuable hands on experience with Pre-K-5 children, making connections, communicating, cooperating and collaborating with educators who are committed to educating the WHOLE child.
- We just conducted workshops for all the teachers at Yalesville and Highland schools on adding physical activity to their classrooms. We combined the academics with physical activity. Some teachers have indicated that they have already started using the techniques and games that were introduced.
- Third grades at Pond Hill School (Wallingford) are doing the ABC for Fitness breaks. Quinnipiac University occupational therapy

and physician's assistant students have been implementing the ABCs for Fitness program (as well as Nutrition Detectives) in 3rd grade classrooms this past semester. The physical education teacher at the school is coordinating the QU students and classroom teachers.

West Hartford, CT. Charter Oak International Academy

The Physical Education Teacher at Charter Oak International Academy provides these examples of statements from teachers in his school:

- **2nd Grade Classroom Teacher**: "When we are sitting on the rug too long we might do a movement activity/song like "Aroostasha," "Joe and the Butter Factory," or "1,2, 3, 4" to get them moving. They have to get into the middle of the circle 1 at a time and do a crazy move while everyone sings. Joe and the butter factory is a song where kids start adding body parts one at a time and moving them around in a circle."

- **A Special Ed Teacher says,** "Even in my small groups my friends need movement. I use body motions and American Sign Language and a little bit of brain gym to help students will expressive and receptive language, to teach meanings of key vocabulary, to memorize numeric patterns (i.e. quarters that equal a dollar- you can ask the fifth graders to do the 25,50,75, a dollar dance), and I link hand movements to vowel sounds. I also use movement by having students leave their work at their space, then rotate to correct peer work."

- **5th Grade Classroom Teacher:** "Sometimes I will do simple exercises to get kids moving and reenergized along the lines of Simon Says. They have to follow what I do and often times I make it silly. They love it. I also have them act out various vocabulary words with their bodies such as parallel lines, perpendicular lines, and we make human number lines. We skip or walk along the line as we skip count."

- **5th Grade Classroom Teacher**: "Since taking over the class is really like beginning the year together, we needed to do some team-building and bonding. We also have a long stretch of academics in the morning, so we take a dance break. We just made it simple with each student adding one movement, then repeating back from the beginning. I like that it works as a memory exercise as well a physical one."

- Art Teacher: "In the art room I use physical/kinesthetic components to help students understand (and for me to assess) and apply concepts of horizontal, vertical and diagonal by having them hold their arms in the given position. I use "Simon Says" with movement to gather attention and transition to hallway or to work tables. When classes are fidgety or tired I use stretching and breathing exercises. When I am teaching drawing the figure, I have students take the pose they want to draw to work out the physical/visual relationships of the arm-body-leg-etc. relationships. There is more, but I probably cannot think of it all at the moment. None of this is heavy cardio vascular stuff, but a moment of movement can make for an hour of happier learning--- and movement is a great way to make intellectual concepts concrete and relatable."

- **3rd Grade Teacher:** "I've been doing some yoga for kids (10-15 minutes) in the morning or to start our afternoon a couple of days during the week. Also, we'll stretch during transitions, do pushups, hold plank. I can add sit-ups to help with your testing. In addition, I try to move students to different parts of the room during lessons for instructional purposes and to provide physical breaks, i.e. start on rug, move to desks for partner work, move to floor whole group, finally go back to desks, etc. There are also body cues to match learning rules, i.e. the cha-cha-cha to remember parts of a word problem (we do it in a conga line)."

- **More from teachers at Charter Oak**: "Every morning we count and we exercise. Each group of tens brings a different movement. (ex: 70's = hopping, 80's =jumping jacks, 90's = sit-ups)" "We dance for transitions."

Chapter 8

Resources

Resources create the bulk of understanding surrounding particular subject matter and help teachers greatly because it backs the subject matter up. Resources help students understand the object of the lesson being conveyed. Without resources the whole teacher-learner relationship could be boring and there would be no information to back up what the teacher is delivering. Resources provide the questions that follow the curriculum and provide an in depth understanding of the topic (Copus, R. retrieved from Google, Blurt It, July 8. 2013).

School districts need to select adapt and develop a variety of resources to support student learning. Effective use of resources will help students to absorb what they have learned and create knowledge for themselves and develop strategies and skills for learning in the 21st century. It is advisable to build an abundant stock of resources such as the ones we have provided for you. in order to help your PASS initiative get off the ground. Conducting in-house workshops that provide teachers with the opportunity to demonstrate and/or share experiences with resources can be a good way to better understand what is available and utilized within the school district. We have taken the time to put the many excellent resources and references that are out there in one place for easy usage. Feel free to adopt, adjust, and make them your own and most importantly use them often! When selecting resources the following principles should be considered:

- They should be in line with the Learning Outcomes in the Syllabus.
- They should take students' prior knowledge into account
- They should present concepts and ideas in an active and effective way.
- They should engage students actively in learning.
- They should provide knowledge but also scaffold learning.
- They should provide for students' differences by offering varied learning activities at different levels of difficulty.
- Resources used to complement textbooks should promote and extend independent learning in addition to what was learned in class.
- They should facilitate discussion and enquiry.

Provided by: Project Math's-Learning and Teaching for the 21st Century

Resources for Classroom Teachers
Lesson Ideas Active Academics provides practical ideas for integrating physical activity in K-5 math, reading/language arts, health/nutrition, and physical education classes.
www.activeacademics.org

Take 10 offers a searchable database of classroom-based physical activity lessons for K-5.
www.take10.net/whatistake10.asp?page=new

Activity Bursts for the Classroom shows elementary schools how to restructure physical activity into multiple, brief episodes throughout the day without taking away valuable time for classroom instruction.
www.davidkatzmd.com/abcforfitness.aspx

Brain Breaks provides physical activity lessons for K-6 classrooms. Lesson menu is broken into specific content areas and other settings.
www.emc.cmich.edu/brainbreaks/

Energizers are classroom based physical activities for grades K-8 that integrate physical activity with academic concepts.
www.ncpe4me.com/energizers.html

Winter Kids Outdoor Learning Curriculum is aligned with National Education Standards and offers interdisciplinary lessons in a variety of subjects for grades K-12 with a complete adapted component for disabled children.
www.winterkids.org

Action Based Learning - puts brain-based learning into action with teacher friendly, "kid-tested, kid-approved" strategies that move students to learn! See the "articles" tab.
http://www.actionbasedlearning.com/

Brain Rules - is a multimedia resource detailing 12 key rules scientists know about how the brain works. For each brain rule Dr. John Medina presents the science and then offers ideas for investigating how the rule might apply to our daily lives, especially at work and school
http://www.brainrules.net

"Spark, the Revolutionary New Science of Exercise and the Brain"
by Dr. John Ratey
This book presents groundbreaking research linking the connection between exercise and the brain's performance. Evidence shows how even moderate exercise will supercharge mental circuits to beat stress, sharpen thinking, enhances memory, and much more. Chapter two is dedication to physical activity and education.
http://www.johnratey.com

Organizations Supporting Youth Physical Activity and Wellness

National Association for Sport and Physical Education
www.aahperd.org/naspe/

CDC's Division of Adolescent and School Health
www.cdc.gov/healthyyouth/index.htm

Alliance for a Healthier Generation
www.healthiergeneration.org/

Action for Healthy Kids
www.actionforhealthykids.org/

Resources for implementing PASS During the School Day

Implementing Classroom-Based Physical Activity

Instant Recess Lift Off!- activity videos.

Just-A-Minute (JAM) School Program-fitness break activities, including monthly newsletter.

Maximizing Opportunities for Physical Activity during the School Day

Mississippi's Health in Action Program

Mississippi's You've Gotta Move Program

Moving More Challenge - fitness challenge program available to schools to encourage physical activity before/during/after school.

NASPE's Teacher Toolbox

North Carolina Energizers - download "booklets" of energizer activities for elementary and middle school classrooms.

nrgBalance

nrgOutdoors
nrg Powered by Choice-for teens and leaders.

PE Central

Physical Activity Used as Punishment and/or Behavior Management (2009)

Ready, Set, Fit –health and activity program for classroom teachers in grades 3 and 4.

Take 10! ®

U.F.A. Brain Breaks- brain break activities

Ultimate Camp Resource

Yoga Recess in Schools-DVD and free training

10 Simple Activities to Encourage Physical Activity in the Classroom

ABC for Fitness

Accelerated Learning Brain Breaks - unusual brain break games.

Active Academics - activities integrate physical activity into lessons, by grade and subject.

Activity Ideas for All Seasons

Behavior Matters Brain Breaks - brain break activities.

Brain Breaks- elementary level, organized by academic subject matter.

California Project Lean-Jump Start Teens

CDC Health and Academics

Choosy Kids – Resources for nutrition and physical activity.

Circus Fit

Comprehensive School Physical Activity Programs (2008)

Dr. Jean Brain Breaks - list of activities for younger children (pre-school and K).

Dr. Jean Songs and Activities for Young Children

Energizers: Classroom Based Activities –printable activity cards.

Fit Kids Activities - physical activities that integrate academics.

Fitness Fun Forever

Game On! The Ultimate Wellness Challenge

Get Up and Go!

Resources for PASS Before and After School

A Primer on Joint Use

A Running Start-video resource for coaching youth runners

Afterschool.gov

Afterschool Counts!

After School Physical Activity Website

BAM: Body and Mind

Considerations for Developing Effective Afterschool Programs

California's After School Physical Activity Guidelines

Carolina Panthers Fit Squad Activity Videos

Co-Curricular Physical Activity and Sport Programs for Middle School Students (2002)

Fit for Life After-School Program – activity leader handouts and nutrition mini-lessons.

Games Kids Play

The Healthy Kids, Healthy New York After-School Initiative Toolkit

Joint Use

Kidnetic

Walking and Biking to School

Bike for All

CDC Walk to School Program

Creating a Walk to School Program

International Walk to School Program

Safe Routes to School

Walking School

Additional Resources for PASS

Assessing Recess: Growing Concerns about Shrinking Play Time in Schools

Games Kids Play

International Play Association Promoting Recess

KaBoom! *Play Matters* Report

Maximizing Recess Physical Activity

North Carolina See, Learn, Do Recess Activity Videos

Playworks Education Energized: The 2009-2010 Playbook

ProTeacher Indoor Recess Games

Recess before Lunch Resources

Recess for Elementary School Students (2006)

School Recess and Group Classroom Behavior-article about positive relationship between recess and improved classroom behavior

Sixty Alternatives to Withholding Recess

UNC School of Education-Importance of Recess

Yoga Recess in Schools-DVD and free training

References

American Alliance of Health, Physical Education, Recreation, and Dance. (1975).
AAHPERD's physical best guidelines. Reston, VA.

American College of Sports Medicine. (2000). *ACSM's guidelines for exercise testing and prescription* (6th ed.). Philadelphia: Lippincott, Williams, & Wilkins.

Berg, K. (2010) *Justifying Physical Education Based on Neuroscience Evidence* Journal of Physical Education, Recreation and Dance.81(3): 24-29.

Blaydes, J. (2000) *Action Based Learning: Thinking on Your Feet.* Advocacy: A Case for Daily Quality Physical Education Retrieved 4/25/2010.www.actionbasedlearning.com

Blaydes, J. (1996). *The Body/Mind Connection: It's Implications for Physical Education* Texas Journal of Health, Physical Education, Recreation, and Dance.112 (4): 9-13.

Centers for Disease Control and Prevention. (2001). *Increasing Physical Activity: A report on recommendations of the task force on community preventive services.* Morbidity and Mortality Weekly Report 50: 1-14.

Diamond, M. (1998). *Magic Trees of the Mind.* Zephyr Press. Brookline, MA.

Dwyer, T., Sallis, J.F., Blizzard, L., Lazarus, R., & Dean, K. (2001). Relation of Academic Performance to Physical Activity and Fitness in Children. *Pediatric Exercise Science*, 13: 225-238.

Gage, F. (1999). *New Nerve Cells for the Adult Br*ain, Scientific American, May, p.48.

Gardner, H. (1999). *Eight Multiple Intelligences*, retrieved 11/20/2010. http://expectumf.umf.maine.edu

Gardner, H. (1983). *Frames of Mind.* New York: Basic Books

Gilbert, A. (2000). *Brain Dance.* Creative Dance Center, Seattle, WA. Retrieved 1/26/2008
www.creativedance.org

Glasser, W. (1965) *Reality Therapy and Choice Theory* (1998). Retrieved 1/29/2011
www.associatedcontent.com/article/404351/an_overview_of_dr

Groppel, J. (2011). *Thinking Beyond the Field: Leading Change in Your Community.* Keynote address: American Alliance of Health, Physical Education, Recreation and Dance. San Diego, CA.

Hannaford, C. (1995*). Smart moves: Why learning is not all in the head.* Marshall, NC: Great Ocean

Jensen, E. (2000). *Learning with the Body in Mind: The Scientific Basis for Energizers, Movement, Play, Games, and Physical Education.* Corwin Press: Thousand Oaks, CA.

Jensen, E. (1998). <u>Teaching with the Brain in Mind</u>. Turning Point Publishing:New Orleans, LA.

Katz, D. L. (2007) *ABC's for Fitness: A Teachers Manual.* Retrieved 4/21/2011 http://www.davidkatzmd.com/docs/ ABC_for_Fitness_publication_2010.pdf

Kuczla, M. (2010) *The Kinesthetic Classroom.* Program session at the AAHPERD convention. Indianapolis, IN.

Lengel, T. & Kuczala, M. (2010). *The Kinesthetic Classroom: Teaching and Learning through Movement.* Corwin Press: Thousand Oaks, CA.

Mitchell, D. & Scheuer, L.J.(2003). Does Physical Activity Influence Academic Performance? In *The New P.E. & Sports Dimension* retrieved March 3, 2010 from SportaPolis. www.sports-media.org/sportapolisnewsletter19.htm

NASPE. (2011). National Association for Sport and Physical Education Position Statement:
Physical Education is Critical to Educating the Whole Child. NASPE is a division of the American Alliance for Health, Physical Education, Recreation, and Dance. Pp.1-9.

Olshansky, S.J. (2005). A potential decline in life expectancy in the United States in the 21st century. *New England Journal of Medicine,* 352 (11): 1138-1145.

Ratey, J. (2008). *Spark: The Revolutionary New Science of Exercise and the Brain.* Little Brown and Company: New York, NY.

U.S. Department of Health and Human Services. (1996). Center for Disease Control, *Physical activity and health: A report of the Surgeon General--At glance.*
Atlanta: U.S. Department of Health and Human Services, Centers for Disease Control and Prevention, National Center for Chronic Disease Prevention and Health Promotion. Atlanta: Author.

U.S. Department of Health and Human Services. (1997). *Healthy people 2000.* Centers for Disease Control and Prevention, National Center for Chronic Disease Prevention and Health Promotion. Atlanta: Author.

U.S. Department of Health and Human Services. (2000). *Healthy people 2010—conference Edition: Physical activity and fitness* (22). Atlanta: Author.

U.S. Department of Health and Human Services, (2004). Centers for Disease Control and Prevention, National Center for Chronic Disease Prevention and Health Promotion. Atlanta: Author.

Appendix A

Blank PASS Lesson Plan Template

PASS Lesson Template

Name of Activity:

Safety:	Time:

Facility:
   ❐ Classroom   ❐ Multipurpose
     ❐ Gymnasium   ❐ Outdoors
	Equipment:

Physical Activity Level:
   ❐ Light   ❐ Moderate   ❐ Vigorous
	Type of Activity:
	  ❐ Brain Break/Energizer ❐ Content Rich
	                 ❐ Fun

Common Core Connection:

Activity Description:

Grade Level Modifications:

Printed in the United States
By Bookmasters